DATE DUE			

The Theatrical Designs of
Charles Ricketts

Theater and Dramatic Studies, No. 23

Oscar G. Brockett, Series Editor

Leslie Waggener Professor of Fine Arts
and Professor of Drama
The University of Texas at Austin

Bernard Beckerman, Series Editor, 1980-1983

Brander Matthews Professor of Dramatic Literature
Columbia University in the City of New York

Other Titles in This Series

The Theatrical Designs of
Charles Ricketts

by
Eric Binnie
Assistant Professor of
Performing Arts and English
Colby College
Waterville, Maine

UMI RESEARCH PRESS
Ann Arbor, Michigan

Produced and distributed by
UMI Research Press
an imprint of
University Microfilms International
A Xerox Information Resources Company
Ann Arbor, Michigan 48106

Library of Congress Cataloging in Publication Data

Binnie, Eric.
The theatrical designs of Charles Ricketts.

(Theater and dramatic studies ; no. 23)
Revision of the author's thesis (doctoral—University
of Toronto).
Bibliography: p.
Includes index.
1. Ricketts, Charles S., 1866-1931.   2. Theaters—
Stage-setting and scenery.   I. Title.   II. Series

PN2096.R5B56   1984   792'.025'0924   84-23921
ISBN 0-8357-1584-1 (alk. paper)

For Ann

Charles Shannon, *Man with a Greek Vase*
Portrait of Charles Ricketts at age thirty-five.

The main body of Charles Ricketts' life-work is in permanent media which will ensure his fame lasting as long as any fame can last in this world, but his work for the theatre was considerable and important, and he put his wonderful powers into it as wholly as into any other branch of his art, so that as complete a record of it as possible is most desirable in all its supreme beauty.

Gordon Bottomley, 1932

Contents

List of Figures

Acknowledgments

A study of this nature would have been impossible without the help of many museums, libraries and art galleries, besides holders of individual private collections of Ricketts' materials. I wish to thank all of the institutions listed in Appendix B (A Finding List of Ricketts' Designs), together with the University of Toronto Rare Book Room, the British Library Department of Manuscript Acquisitions, the Toronto Public Library Theatre Department, the University of Bristol Drama Department Library, the National Gallery of Canada, the National Gallery of Ireland, the Witt Library of the Courtauld Institute, the Enthoven Collection of the Victoria and Albert Museum, and the British Theatre Museum. For giving me access to private materials, designs and information I wish to express my thanks to Anne Yeats, Ann Saddlemyer, Cecil Lewis, Liam Miller, Carl Woodring and Charles Gullans.

I wish to thank my former professors at the Graduate Centre for the Study of Drama, at the University of Toronto, for their patient support and helpful suggestions as I prepared the original form of this study. The early part of my research was generously supported by a Canada Council Doctoral Fellowship. In preparing the manuscript for publication I received the support of a Swarthmore College Faculty Research Grant and the invaluable secretarial help of Thelma Miller, Helen DiFeliciantonio, Ellen Dolski, Helene McCann and Joann Massary.

In describing various designs and photographs I have used brackets to indicate uncertainty of attribution. Throughout my discussion of productions I have used the modern term "director," though in the British theatre during the period of Ricketts' work for the stage, the term "producer" or even "manager" would have been more common.

1

Ricketts and His Times

The milieu of Charles Ricketts has been so frequently subjected to a knowing condescension that it has become difficult to separate the artist from the insubstantial figure swathed in a mauve decadence, the working craftsman from the aesthete. Even a sympathetic writer like Sir Kenneth Clark, who sets out to praise Ricketts, quickly descends to the vaguely dismissive tone:

> He was a painter, sculptor, book illustrator and stage designer of real distinction, and much of his work, especially his sculpture and his costume designs, will be "rediscovered" with astonishment.

One might reasonably expect this to lead into a close analysis of the sculpture and costume designs, perhaps even some instructive comparison between these two forms of three-dimensional creativity. But Sir Kenneth's love of the telling phrase, his penchant for the panoramic vision, sweeps him back from any precise criticism, and he continues:

> The quintessence of the nineties, he came at the exact point of juncture between the pre-Raphaelites and the symbolists, the point at which Beardsley emerged corruptly from the virtuous Burne-Jones.

One might expect some explanation of the chaste Ricketts' unexpected midwifery in this titillating nativity scene. For interpretation Sir Kenneth is reduced to anecdote:

> When he was offered the post of director of the National Gallery he made it a condition that all the pictures must be reframed, the floors covered with Persian rugs and the rooms filled with flowers.[1]

To be fair one should point out that this account of Ricketts is given in Sir Kenneth's autobiography and not in a scholarly study, but the progression of thought in the three consecutive statements is sufficient to make the point that Ricketts' life, his personality and, indeed, his own love of anecdote, often tend to obscure his artistic achievement.

The larger souls of his own generation, men and women of wit, capable of self-mockery as well as the pointed mock, give an altogether different picture of Ricketts: that of a man of painstaking exactitude, of wide-ranging expertise, of vision, devotion and nobility. For example, George Bernard Shaw, a man given as much to exaggerated praise as to vaulting scorn, wrote of Ricketts' designs for the Don Juan in Hell episode from *Man and Superman:*

> It seems to me that we (I say "we" much as an organ-blower uses the plural pronoun when speaking of the organist's performance of a Bach Fugue) hit on a most valuable and fascinating stage convention.[2]

Shaw's correspondence from this period is full of the delights of Ricketts' designs for this production, but it is the playwright's self-abnegation vis-à-vis the designer that is of particular interest here because it typifies the very substantial impression which Ricketts made among men of creativity and perception.

It was through his early work as a wood-engraver, illustrator and designer of fonts and book bindings that Ricketts first became acquainted with the writers, artists and aesthetes of the fin-de-siècle such as Oscar Wilde, Laurence Binyon, William Orchardson, William Rothenstein and Bernard Berenson.[3] Among this circle Ricketts was exceptional in several respects. A practicing craftsman, apprenticed from the age of fifteen, and almost entirely dependent upon his skills for survival, he must have seemed, even then, to have had a hard, practical sense, an economy of means in art as in life, rare enough among his associates. In later years, Oscar Wilde would often joke about the frugal, but willing, hospitality of suppers at the Vale, where Ricketts shared a studio apartment with his companion, Charles Hazelwood Shannon, the lithographer and portrait-painter.[4]

Ricketts' background would also have made him strange to his fellows, in that he was a European, born in Geneva in 1866, the son of an English naval officer and a lady of Italian/French ancestry. He grew up and was educated, mostly by governesses, in London and on the Continent. When his mother's health failed he accompanied her abroad, and he was accustomed to attend musical, operatic and dramatic productions regularly from his earliest years. Even in a relatively small provincial center such as Boulogne, where he spent some time as an adolescent, he found well-attended, subsidized theatres and a kind of audience receptive to theatre rather than to theatrical stars. Such conditions would have been far to seek in the British Isles before the Irish dramatic renaissance in the late 1890s.

Ricketts' interest in theatrical decoration dates from early in his life, though the first evidence of his practical involvement in the theatre dates from his fortieth year. The diary entry for 27 January 1901 tells us that the subject of stage design "has haunted me for years."[5] Throughout his life he studied and appreciated music, drama, painting, sculpture and antiquities. His taste was wide-ranging, though his judgment of the post-Impressionists would now be considered severe if not reactionary. He was a connoisseur of Japanese, Greek, Persian, Egyptian and European art, frequently consulted by other experts, by galleries and private collectors to date and verify works of art. A major project of his later years was the advisory work he undertook in the establishment of the new National Gallery of Canada in Ottawa. He remained the gallery's European buyer and advisor till the end of his life, and is directly responsible for the purchase of many of its finest Renaissance acquisitions and, less commendably, for the relative paucity of its post-Impressionist works. Ricketts was conversant with the major European languages and traveled extensively in Europe and the Near East. Together with Shannon he built up, from very modest means, a considerable private collection of paintings and antiquities, most of which now form part of the British national collection, especially in the Fitzwilliam Museum, Cambridge, and the Victoria and Albert Museum, London. In this astute building of the collection Ricketts reveals another aspect of his practical nature, though the works of art were never bought with an eye to investment.

Ricketts' diaries tell us of his excitement over each new discovery, be it a Persian miniature lying forgotten in some junk wagon, some new sensation at the theatre, or some new book he has found especially delightful. His curiosity was catholic and he read widely, especially in French and English literature. Montaigne, Baudelaire and Shakespeare were perennial favorites but, when some newly discovered work pleased him, he would return to it again and again.

Besides his major studies of *Titian* and *The Art of the Prado*, Ricketts wrote several essays on art and design, kept diaries for many years, and entered into a lively and prolonged correspondence with many of the outstanding men and women of his times. He and Shannon entertained in a modest but stylish manner. The visits of literary and artistic leaders of the day, such as W.B. Yeats, Edward Gordon Craig, H.G. Wells and Léon Bakst are recorded in the diaries. Ricketts also had time for the less celebrated. On the one hand, he was always hospitable and encouraging to the very young, being one of the first to appreciate the drawings of Augustus John and Paul Nash. On the other hand, he was patient and understanding with the very old; throughout his busy years at the Vale he always had time to take the aged painter, Alphonse Legros, on excursions to museums and exhibitions. Because of his lasting interest in the arts of the previous generation Ricketts became a kind of repository of facts and stories about artists like Gustave Moreau, Auguste Rodin, Dante Gabriel Rossetti, such authors as Feodor Dostoyevsky, Ivan Turgenev, Friedrich Nietzsche, such musicians as Richard Wagner and Gioacchino Rossini. From anecdote, correspondence and personal knowledge of the artistic giants of the previous generation, Ricketts became, in his own maturity, a natural source of information for the writers and artists of the next.

Yet it would be misguided to see Ricketts as a kind of English Goncourt, providing a literary and artistic salon for his contemporaries. The diaries indeed show that he led a very full social life and knew most of "little London." In some periods he dined out and attended theatres or musical concerts as often as four times a week. Yet he was also a very private person who worked long and painstakingly at his several artistic pursuits, frequently agonizing over his lack of achievement, his financial insecurity, and the apathy of the British public towards art and artists. Apart from his contribution to the history of stage design, which forms the main part of this study, he had little popular success in any of his various fields of endeavor—engraving, book design, painting, modeling—though in each of these arts he has been deservedly praised by informed critics. Perhaps he spread himself among too many different branches of art, and relied too much for guidance upon the study of great paintings from the past. He suggests as much himself when he describes himself and Shannon as being

> like tapestry weavers who weave from behind. I have often felt more like a tracer than an artist. A copyist, after all, analyses the processes and mental mechanism behind the work he is copying.[6]

Thomas Sturge Moore suggests that Ricketts' range of abilities detracted from his artistic reputation:

> Versatility often stood in his way. Many who had committed themselves to admiration of his early pen compositions, sniffed at his printed books and decorative borders; and those who welcomed the books remained cold to his paintings; and some who had honored his paintings thought his stage work a mere cheapening and popularization, at the expense of those far greater creations.[7]

Though frequently bitter about his neglect by contemporary critics and patrons, Ricketts' awareness of his own limitations led him to bouts of severe self-doubt and depression.

He realized that, given his unique position as a connoisseur, he had missed two great, influential opportunities in his life: his failure to be elected to the Slade Professorship of Fine Arts at Oxford University in 1910, and his own refusal to be nominated for the directorship of the British National Gallery in 1915. In either of these positions he could have usefully employed his extensive learning to educate a younger generation of artists and gallery-visitors towards an understanding of those aesthetic principles he held dear.

The scheme he presented for the Slade series of forty-eight lectures gives an invaluable insight into the bias of Ricketts' attitude to the arts of the past. It is an outline course covering the development of architecture, sculpture and painting, from the decline of Roman art with the emergence of Byzantine influences in the West, up to the present day, that is, 1910. In the introduction to the scheme he writes:

I have, however, given greater prominence to the Art of the Nineteenth Century, since the work of that period must come within the experience of all students.[8]

For an artist who deliberately eschewed the modern and was delighted to be considered a "post-Raphaelite," in the sense of being a late pre-Raphaelite, this is obviously special pleading.[9] It is true that, in general, students are more familiar with the works of the generation immediately prior to their own, and, in fairness to Ricketts, I should also point out that in the scheme of lectures, he extended the principle of accessibility to Oxford itself, always laying great emphasis on works that could be seen in or near the city.

The course is particularly strong on the relationships between the various branches of art, the scope with which Ricketts traces influences between schools of artists, the way in which he relates fine art to literature, and on practical concerns with technical developments in the arts. The bias of his preferences can be judged from the fact that only Michelangelo, Titian, Rembrandt and Turner warrant two lectures each, and great prominence is given to the visionary or ideal qualities of painting, scarcely any to realism. His devotion to the pre-Raphaelites manifests itself in the language used to outline his intended lectures: "Imaginative use of Detail," "Dramatic Intensity and Concentration in Design," "Colour as a means of Poetic Expression," "Narrative in Art," "The Value of Symbolism in Decoration." In describing French art of the nineteenth century he stressed the similarities between Delacroix and the English pre-Raphaelites in their "Tragic Sense in Art," their "Passion for Expressive Colour." Where many of Ricketts' contemporaries, and most modern students, would take exception to his scheme is in his lionizing of the decorative and symbolist painters such as Gustave Moreau and Puvis de Chavannes. The last lecture of all is reserved for the impressionists. The printed lecture heading suggests that Ricketts intended to play safe with mere facts, theories and influences, but his good intentions in this respect must have been too heavy to bear, for he has added in pencil, underlined, "Intimidation in art and criticism." This last phrase refers to Ricketts' oft-expressed opinion that art critics had foisted the works of the Impressionists, and especially of the post-Impressionists, onto a gullible and timid public, with disastrous results to the more conservative painters of his own period.

The professorship was offered, instead, to Ricketts' friend Selwyn Image. This may have been a blessing in disguise, for, a few years later, during the First World War, the professorship was suspended because "art was not important, an occupation of our leisure, that in these serious times, the world could do without."[10] Such a piece of bureaucratic impertinence would have enraged Ricketts at any time, but it was especially distressing in time of war. Though never clearly expressed in the diaries, Ricketts was disturbed by the imbalance in his own nature which, while always sympathetic to human suffering, caused his major concern during the war years to be the prevention of damage to British and European masterpieces of art and architecture. The diaries repeatedly return to the same subject:

1 Sept. 1914 Rubens' *Miraculous Draught of Fishes* reported destroyed. We are filled with anxiety over the Puvis decorations at Amiens and the Cathedral.... A shell falling among the Puvis walls might blot out one-half of his life-work for ever.... The fall of a bomb near the Paris Opera House set me thinking about the possible destruction of the Baudry ceilings, which I value more than I can say. The idea of a War of Vandalism—of a set purpose—staggers me more than incidents of cruelty and brutality, which are, after all, *individual* acts of *limited purpose and range,*

and,

12 Sept. 1914 Destruction of Reims Cathedral.... Reims has been called the Gothic Parthenon, its sculpture represents certainly one-third of the world's store of Gothic work. I am glad that I never saw the building nor its glass,

and,

6 Aug. 1915 When the younger Michael Field was on the point of death her last words were "Not yet, not yet!"—there seemed to her just a frail chance of life. So one thinks of pictures, Greek vases, and books, and hugs the idea that it is "not yet, not yet" the end one dreads.[11]

One can hardly escape the feeling that there is something unwholesome here, and something vaguely troubling to Ricketts, particularly in the last analogy, moving as it does from the incident of a dear friend's death to the perpetual obsession with the possible destruction of works of art. On the other hand, Ricketts proceeded with the things he could do, writing to the press repeatedly about removing art treasures for safekeeping, sandbagging repositories of art which could not be moved, such as Westminster Abbey, concerning himself with what was ultimately a successful appeal to recall the promising young sculptor E.A. Cole from the front line of battle, designing costumes for Lena Ashwell's and Mrs. Penelope Wheeler's productions for soldiers at the war bases, donating paintings to Red Cross sales.

Given Ricketts' sensitivity to the fate of works of art in times of war, it is, perhaps, as well that Selwyn Image and not Charles Ricketts was at first appointed to and later dismissed from the Chair of Fine Art at Oxford. Nevertheless, the scheme of lectures he proposed is a valuable record of information about Ricketts' aesthetic preconceptions and touchstones. It indicates, in a nutshell, his overview of the development of civilization, and, in particular, it points to the major influences of his life and work.

The other great regret of Ricketts' life was that he did not accept the directorship of the National Gallery when this was offered to him in 1915. Since the start of the war he had frequently berated the trustees of the National Gallery about the need to protect its treasures from possible war damage. For example, a letter published in the *Observer,* dated 14 February 1915, ends caustically:

I would urge that the protection of the tombs [in Westminster Abbey] should be entrusted to the engineer who has rendered immune from danger the Albert Memorial, which has so far benefited by attention not vouchsafed to the relics of the Confessor and the tomb of Queen Elizabeth.

Faithfully yours,
Charles Ricketts

P.S. The tardiness of the trustees and guardians of our national treasures should bring before the public (after the war) the instant need of a Minister of Fine Arts, who would be responsible to the nation for the maintenance of efficiency among those answerable for the order and management of our institutions and monuments. The existing state of things renders everybody's duty no man's duty. [12]

Because of such attacks on the officials, Ricketts felt, when first approached on the subject of applying for the directorship, that he would have no chance of being elected. Indeed this was not the case, as the appointment would have come directly from the government not from the civil service or the trustees, and the other two nominees, Charles Holmes and Robert Witt, had volunteered to step down in Ricketts' favor. He records his rather pompous reply:

It is impossible: I am an artist, I could not give up my work to become a Civil Servant and sit in an office. The berth—as it now stands—cannot be undertaken by a man with any sort of personality. [13]

While his reply is headstrong, it is obviously sincere, and has little relationship to the more colorful version given by Sir Kenneth Clark above.

It was eight months later when the folly of Ricketts' hasty decision came home to him:

16 June 1916   Several men in the evening. Yeats among them. He suddenly blurts out that MacColl has told him that I have declined the Directorship of the National Gallery. This causes a sort of sensation among my friends, and for the first time in months I feel something grip my inside. I know that I regret, and shall always regret, my decision; that it would have been a dignified end to my life to have recast, rehung, and revised the dear old place; that I should have risked discomfort and moments of anger. I now believe that I could have gained the necessary ascendency over the Trustees; I have been an ass. [14]

Ricketts came to realize that he, who had so often castigated the British public for its apathy towards art, had missed a great opportunity to put his faith in art to the test. He was guilty of that very fault which he had so often used in the past to condemn the common man:

The deeper-lying evil is the faculty not to act up to conviction, which characterizes the Britisher. He will know that a thing is right, but choose the easier course, because it is more covenient, or even without reason, by a perversion of instinct. [15]

By choosing the easier, more covenient course he avoided the necessity of directly bringing the public, which he so roundly condemned, face to face with that essentially idealistic concept of art which he had inherited from Ruskin, through William Morris and the pre-Raphaelites. It would seem that this traditional, liberal and proselytizing view of art was at odds with an inner, more perverse and exclusive instinct, possibly derived from Huysmans and the Symbolists.

Ricketts' moment of truth, when he realized he had refused a position he should have accepted, is a classic example of the artistic dichotomy of the turn of the century, the years of his prime. On the one hand he desired the influence and power that would have enabled him to project his understanding of the arts of the past into the future. On the other hand he was reluctant to leave the security of his refined existence to meddle in the irksome tasks of public office and bureaucracy. Ultimately the roots of this quandary are moral and political, and they are to be found in Ruskin:

> The great lesson of history is, that all the fine arts hitherto—having been supported by the selfish power of the noblesse, and never having extended their range to the comfort and relief of the mass of the people—the arts...have only accelerated the ruin of the states they adorned;... for in proportion to the nobleness of the power is the guilt of its use for purposes vain and vile; and hitherto the greater the art, the more surely has it been used, and used solely, for the decoration of pride, or the provoking of sensuality. Another course lies open to us.... For us there is the loftier and lovelier privilege of bringing the power and charm of art within the reach of the humble and the poor; and as the magnificence of past ages failed by its narrowness and its pride, ours may prevail and continue by its universality and its lowliness.[16]

There were two main developments from this moral and political position: the pre-Raphaelite and the Symbolist.

William Morris took Ruskin's vision and applied it to the model of a utopian future, based on an idealized medieval past, a past without "the selfish power of the noblesse" as Ruskin had described it. In *The Earthly Paradise* (1866-70) Morris writes:

> Forget six counties overhung with smoke,
> Forget the snorting steam and piston stroke,
> Forget the spreading of the hideous town;
> Think rather of the pack-horse on the down,
> And dream of London, small, and white, and clean.[17]

The pre-Raphaelite painters, such as Holman Hunt and John Everett Millais, painted and popularized this world of contented, equitable craftsmen in a clean, healthy world.

The Symbolist writers and painters reacted against Ruskin's leveling of the arts, and yet they, too, often adopted an ideal, dream setting of medievalism, with the major differences that the landscapes were insubstantial and the figures far from healthy. Indeed they were content to escape from life and all its muddy realities. Some even desired to escape the body altogether. The most famous statement of this school is Villiers de l'Isle-Adam's character Axël, in the play of the same name (1855-56):

> Live? No. Our existence is full—and its cup is running over. . . . The future?—Sara, believe what I say: we have just consumed the future. . . . It is the earth, don't you see, that has become the Illusion! Admit, Sara, that in our strange hearts we have destroyed the love of life—and it is indeed in *reality* that we ourselves have become our souls! To agree to live after that would be but a sacrilege against ourselves. Live? Our servants will do that for us. . . . I have thought so much, I would not deign to act.[18]

Others of the Symbolists desired an artificial world surrounded by beautiful objects and sensations. The most influential statement of this idea was Huysmans' novel *A Rebours* (1884) whose hero, des Esseintes, is usually taken as typical of this, the artificial or decadent school of symbolism:

> Le tout est . . . de savoir concentrer son esprit sur un seul point, de savoir s'abstraire suffisamment pour amener l'hallucination et pouvoir substituer le rêve de la réalité à la réalité même.[19]

The concept that an ideal of beauty might become, or replace, reality is a tendency we also find noted in relation to Ricketts' artistic beliefs:

> Not only to create beauty, but to find it and set off its structure seemed to him [Ricketts] so essentially a part of the artist's duty, that he could not forgive Holbein for painting anyone as ugly as Archbishop Warham, or credit Erasmus's praise of that prelate's learning, virtue and intelligence. And the portrait of a man with a bulbous nose in the Prado, counted against the same master as though his sitter's defect had been his invention; Raphael would not have accepted the commission.[20]

But Ricketts did not hold with all aspects of the Symbolists. He had too much love of life, too much sense of humor to aspire to Axël's deliquescent ambitions. Yet Ricketts was influenced both by the Symbolists, whom he knew and admired in Paris, and by the pre-Raphaelite handcraft tradition in which he had been schooled at the old City and Guilds School of Art in Lambeth. The main body of his work lies somewhere between the two schools of thought. His image of himself would seem to vacillate between the figure of a benign craftsman and erudite instructor, and the neglected aesthete withdrawing from life into a precious shell.

Typical of the many existing accounts of the Ricketts and Shannon household is that of the painter Jacques-Emile Blanche:

> Their flat was filled with exquisite things, Persian miniatures, Tanagra figures, Egyptian antiques, jewels and medals, which millionaires had overlooked. For genuine collectors are poor, they are seekers and men of knowledge guided by their taste.

As soon as the hall door opened one felt an air of culture and refinement in the surprising and eclectic choice of drawings by Turner, Hokusai, Gainsborough, J.F. Millet and Daumier. There was an early water-colour, a *Mort d'Arthur*, by Rossetti, with colouring like Limoges enamel. The keynote of the studio was Rossetti and it was there that I met the last survivor of the William Morris gatherings.

In a white and gold drawing-room with a set of chairs of rather pretentious elegance there were shells, corals, and other sea treasures lying in crystal bowls in which floated cyclamen petals.[21]

It is, perhaps, difficult to imagine the custodian of this ivory tower taking up public office, but, on reflection, who would be better qualified than a careful private collector to become director of the National Gallery?

Ricketts himself was well aware of the tensions within his personality. Throughout his life he used Nietzsche as a kind of grotesque mirror image of his own beliefs, a gauge with which to measure his worst fears about his own aesthetic isolationism:

Years ago when I first read him I was half-frightened to find in print so many things which I felt personally, and to hear them from a mouth I loved so little.[22]

Fifteen years later, shortly before he was offered the directorship he refers to Nietzsche again:

I do not for a moment hold with the Nietzsche idea that art requires slaves, or that it is aristocratic in the mechanical or political sense; art is something else, it is outside life, it is essentially and profoundly non-democratic.... There is no doubt that the artist is temperamentally an "outsider" even when, by chance, he seems most at one with his own times, he worships appearances when the normal man longs for reality. There is jealousy unconfessed on the part of the public, jealousy that this man should be different and perhaps superior.[23]

Ricketts appears to reject Nietzsche yet his life moved increasingly towards a mechanically aristocratic life, surrounded by rare and precious objects.

While still students, Ricketts and Shannon had been the leading lights of the Lambeth Sketch Club, which brought them into contact with other artists and with a range of artistic activities wider than their first discipline of wood engraving. T. Sturge Moore has left an account of the Sketch Club in his preface to *Charles Ricketts R.A.: Sixty-Five Illustrations*. Apart from the sketching, the club provided Ricketts with a pulpit from which to instruct the acolytes in the appreciation of his gods:

Paul Baudry, Puvis de Chavannes, Gustave Moreau, Rossetti, Watts, Flaubert, Zola, Sarah Bernhardt, Wagner, Chopin, Berlioz, Carpeaux, Rodin were then the most admired, but [also] the best work of hundreds more. We went to the library at South Kensington [now the Victoria and Albert Museum] every Saturday evening and saw the art journals and expensive publications, and soon the old masters began to rise like peaks over the foothills, but never became an exclusive object of study.... He had canvassed the work of Gauguin, Van Gogh,

Cézanne, Rimbaud and Mallarmé, before those who wrote them up in this country had heard of them. But no fashion ever imposed on him. He never accepted or rejected artists, movements and periods wholesale. His admiration was alive, not theoretical. Nobody was ever more loyal to experience. His sudden admissions that he had been wrong disconcerted us, not him.[24]

From wood engraving and book illustration it was a natural step to printing and binding. Ricketts founded the Vale Press in 1896. Between then and 1904 when fire destroyed most of his stock he devised three new fonts of type and printed about sixty fine books, often designing the covers himself. Though they never brought great financial returns in their day, these books are now collectors' items. Of the engravings and book designs which formed the serious work of this, the Vale Press period, Gordon Bottomley wrote years later, by way of instruction, to the young artist Paul Nash:

If you have many chances of seeing the work of great imaginative draughtsmen, they can help you greatly. Rossetti's early pen drawings and his Tennyson illustrations, C.S. Ricketts' illustrations to *The Sphinx* and to Lord de Tabley's *Poems* and to *Daphnis & Cloe* all seem to me perfect, especially in the making it clear that the greatest mystery comes from the greatest definiteness and that wonder comes from being cetain about things. Perhaps Ricketts' finest drawing is the "Oedipus and the Sphinx" in the *Pageant* of 1896.[25]

The editors of the above correspondence comment that the doctrine of mystery in definition influenced Nash deeply.[26] In a subsequent letter Bottomley comments on Ricketts' design for his anthology, *King Lear's Wife and Other Plays:*

The design of my book has suffered because the rise in cost of production made it impossible for it to be blocked in gold on vellum as it was intended to be; but even allowing for the resulting unfair meagreness I am well content with it, for it was done by the greatest designer now in the world and it seems to me to show that in every line; he was the first man to achieve that significance of form which everyone tries for now.[27]

Bibliophiles often regret Ricketts' passing from book design to other forms of art, but, it was undoubtedly an unrewarding career financially, and, as Bottomley's comment on the necessity of changing from vellum to grey cardboard indicates, the times were past for the publication of fine books in the Kelmscott tradition. In its own limited way it had been a great tradition, and Ricketts provided a fitting and memorable conclusion:

Think also how, not to mention his designs for May Morris to embroider, this man had designed three founts of type, innumerable initials and decorations, and seconded Morris in his revival of book production, so as to bring tears of admiration into his [Morris'] eyes when on his death-bed he was shown the Vale books, and turned them over and over.[28]

Late in his career, in 1928, and seven years after Shannon, Ricketts was elected a Royal Academician, an honor which he grudgingly accepted. Despite his growing isolation from most of his contemporaries in the world of art, he agreed to becoming an R.A. because of what he believed Burlington House had stood for in the past; a tradition which glorifed, among others less worthy, the great English draftsmen he venerated; Reynolds, Turner, Watts. Childish as the Royal Academy's political machinations seemed to Ricketts, he saw in it a potential source of elevating and honoring what was best in art, and he believed that his being a Royal Academician gave him a public voice, though not, unfortunately, that sway and esteem which elevation to L'Académie Francaise had given, in France, to Anatole France, in the days of Ricketts' youth. It is remarkable that as an elderly man Ricketts could accept this empty honor, while, eleven years earlier, in the prime of life, he had lacked the courage to accept the much more meaningful and influential position of director of the National Gallery.

Ricketts' oil paintings, which he considered his major works, have a certain rarified, otherworldly, often moonlit, atmosphere. Remarkable for the great skill used in handling oils and varnishes to achieve a translucent, glowing surface, and for a rigorous command of line and composition, the paintings tend towards narrative and historic subject matter in a melancholy or tragic mood; at best, haunting and lyrical, at worst, dull and labored. Ricketts' lifelong friend and colleague William Rothenstein, to whom we are indebted for the best-known portrait-lithograph of Ricketts and Shannon, evaluates Ricketts' paintings in relation to his era:

> Was it not Matthew Arnold who observed that great work needs the man and the ripe time? I remember Ricketts saying how embarassing it would be if a great painter suddenly appeared; how foolish we should feel, what poor figures we should cut! Ricketts was quick to respond to so much that was excellent in the arts; no one more sensitive and intelligent. If he and Shannon were not men of genius, at least they knew what company to frequent; if there was no great painter alive to take them as apprentices they could at least apprentice themselves to the best masters of the past. Highly gifted as they were, like the rest of us, they belonged to a period of decline. I think that Ricketts in his heart knew this. With his acute intelligence, his appreciation of the early works of Rossetti and Burne-Jones, of Watts and Whistler, of Delacroix, Daumier and Puvis de Chavannes he must have measured Shannon's and his own work in relation to these. At the same time he knew that, compared with their immediate contemporaries, they stood for a more dignified, a richer content, a more scholarly use of their material.[29]

Considering the weight of his traditional idealism, it is hardly surprising to discover that Ricketts' method of painting was agonizingly slow, laborious and reflective, as Thomas Lowinsky reveals in an interesting comparison between Ricketts' approach to designing for the theatre and his disposition towards easel painting:

Ricketts always felt happy when designing for the theatre. He invented with speed, often finishing whole "sets" with their accompanying dresses in a few hours. He did not enjoy this freedom when painting. Indeed, notwithstanding his skill, he often sat in front of a picture for two or three days before daring to add another touch.[30]

It is not unusual for established painters to turn their attentions to designing for the stage. In the previous century Burne-Jones had designed *King Arthur,* and Sir Lawrence Alma-Tadema a famous *Coriolanus,* both for Henry Irving at the Lyceum. The sets of these two productions were painted by Hawes Craven (1837-1910), perhaps the best-known scene-painter of his generation. He was also a designer and stage-inventor in his own right, but, for the most part, he was content to execute the designs of other artists. Until his time, scene-painters had been employed by theatre managers on a salaried basis. Hawes Craven found it more profitable to rent studios for himself and work on contract, often for several managers at the same time. This became the established pattern of scene painting in the London theatres so that, inevitably, the gulf between a playwright's idea and what actually appeared on stage was widened. In general, sets became increasingly standardized into such categories as "a forest glade," "a market square," "a ruined chapel," and the idea of total artistic control, such as had been advocated and demonstrated in isolated British instances by such actor-managers as Madame Vestris, Charles Macready and Henry Irving, had all but disappeared from the London stage.[31]

With the development of the art theatre societies at the turn of the century, economic necessity led to a breaking of the pattern established by Hawes Craven. What is remarkable, in the case of Ricketts' work for the stage, is that here was an established artist who was concerned, in the first instance, not with the design of elaborate settings and costumes for the large, commercial theatres, but with the early, impecunious efforts of the "new," "poetic" or "serious" drama groups arising out of the enthusiasms and creativity of his literary friends, such as T. Sturge Moore, Laurence Binyon, Gordon Bottomley, George Bernard Shaw and W.B. Yeats. Designers such as Ricketts, working for these new groups, had the opportunity for a greater control of all the visual aspects of production. Indeed, in such a situation, the designer would often have to help realize his own designs, because the society could not afford to pay for specialist labor. This total artistic control corresponded with the ideas Ricketts had culled from his reading about Continental theories of staging, and he brought off some remarkable successes from tiny budgets.

Ricketts had frequented theatres in England and on the Continent since his earliest years. His diaries record his enthusiasm for all types of theatrical presentation. When he liked a particular production he would induce his friends to go too, and he and Shannon often returned four or five times to an especially enjoyable production. Throughout his life he took a childlike delight in the Gilbert and Sullivan operas, in Punch and Judy shows, in pretending to play the pianola, in the early cinema, in fancy dress balls, all of which seem consistent with the habit of revisiting favorite productions many times. He was always keen to see the latest sensation in the theatre: the Japanese plays, the Sicilian actors, the Russian Ballet, the aging Réjane, the visit of Lugné-Poe and the Théâtre de l'Oeuvre. At the same time he was very much ahead of fashion in his study of drama and in his familiarity with the latest experiments and theories of staging. Not only the newest plays excited him: he was greatly interested in attempts to revive the older classics; for example, he found a production of *The Knight of the Burning Pestle* in 1904 "capital," but the audience of a only forty-seven persons "pathetic."[32]

Ricketts had published an article on the subject of stage design in the *Contemporary Review* as early as 1901.[33] The development among his friends and associates of the various theatrical societies for the production of new or serious drama ensured that his ideas would very soon be called into practice, and he was quickly drawn into the work of stage-designer.

The London theatre of the turn of the century can be summarized under two headings; in the commercial west-end theatres there were large-scale, spectacular presentations of mediocre, smart entertainments, often enjoying great financial success and long runs, while in the theatrical societies on the fringes, one could see the fledgling efforts at drama of men of literary talent, or else translations of serious new European plays, presented as cheaply as possible, frequently for no more than one or two afternoon performances. The difference in scale of these two branches of theatre was immense, but, lest it should be suggested that students of the drama tend to overemphasize the importance of the smaller branch, it is apposite to recall George Bernard Shaw's view:

> The change is evident at once. In short, a modern manager need not produce *The Wild Duck;* but he must be very careful not to produce a play which will seem insipid and old-fashioned to playgoers who have seen *The Wild Duck,* even though they may have hissed it.[34]

The productions of such groups as the Independent Theatre (1891-98), The New Century Theatre (1894-1901) and the Literary Theatre Society (1906-07) posed no great threats to the box-office takings of the big theatrical managers, but they did create interest among actors, critics, writers and designers, which, as Shaw suggests, the managers dared not ignore. The theatre-going public continued to flock to lavish productions of *Merrie England* (1902), *The Merry Widow* (1907), *The Quaker Girl* (1910), *Kismet* (1911) and *Chu Chin Chow* (1916).[35] Increasingly, however, serious young actors like Harley Granville Barker, Sybil Thorndike, Lewis Casson and Lena Ashwell were willing to take the risk of appearing in noncommercial plays, and poets like Laurence Binyon, Gilbert Murray, Arthur Symons, Michael Field and John Masefield were willing to put their precious texts to the practical test of stage presentation. More often than not, the plays proved to be dramaturgically weak. Those plays which succeeded were, for the most part, translations from the works of established European dramatists like Ibsen and Maeterlinck. There was no sweeping, revolutionary victory of the "coterie" over the commercial theatres, but, rather, an uneasy truce, with great comings and goings between the two camps, and an air of expectancy, of suspicion even, which ultimately led to a general keenness and a recognition of possibilities. The final outcome was realized in such magnificent compromises as Shaw's *Saint Joan,* albeit some twenty years later. The union of artistic purpose which existed between playwright, actors, director and designer in the artistically, as well as financially, successful production of *Saint Joan* was rare. It was also relatively late in English theatre history because few financially viable productions could gather together a comparable caucus of highly creative artists, each firmly rooted in his individual and well-proven skills, while sharing a common interest in theatrical innovation.

Ricketts' essay "The Art of Stage Decoration," first published in 1901, forms a convenient summary of the major Continental changes in stage presentation at the turn of the century, besides forming a natural and convenient prologue to a study of Ricketts' own designs. Since copies of the essay, in either of its two published forms, are difficult to locate I will quote from it at length.

The essay begins with praise of what Wagner had achieved at Bayreuth; the practical nature of that theatre, its adaptability, its convenience from an audience point of view. Ricketts praises Wagner's general concept of the integration of all aspects of a production into a unified artistic experience. Yet Ricketts felt that the operas suffered from a lack of "the painter's sense of visualising his work beautifully."[36] He dislikes Wagner's love of show, of mechanical dragons, vanishing scenery and fire. He concludes that

If his practical sense was admirable, his pictorial taste was less sure; in fact it was merely a further elaboration of the sham realism current in all opera houses of his time—it was at once literal, complex and trivial. In the very texture of his magnificent tone poems lies a tendency to over-explain, to underline unnecessarily, even to strain his medium by literal imitation; to the sound of horse's hoofs he loved to add the real horse itself, and this tendency affected his conception of stage setting.[37]

This valid criticism shows something of Ricketts' fine understanding of music, as well as of the purely visual.

He finds that Adolphe Appia's reaction against Wagner's "fussy detail" arises, like Ricketts' own criticism, out of a deep love and appreciation of the operas themselves. He approves of Appia's discarding of "literalness of detail," his reduction of settings into

abstract forms [that] have a beauty of their own which is imaginative in mood and therefore suitable to works of the imagination, [his] enveloping effect of ever-changing light, accompanying and interpreting the action like the presence of the music itself.[38]

Using Appia's idea of the multileveled stage floor Ricketts goes on to condemn the standard British stage as "flat," "makeshift," "like the footlights, an economical survival of the eighteenth century."[39]

He uses the designs for the Russian Ballet, particularly those of Léon Bakst, to demonstrate that conventional scenery can also enhance a production:

> His [Bakst's] disregard of reality has a romantic quality, and he may be said to replace Nature by something rather like it which is altogether delightful.[40]

If there is a general principle in Bakst's work it is the use of a highly personal "pitch of colour" together with "the avoidance of realistic shadows and relief." Ricketts comments that his own sense of color, in the earliest designs he executed, such as for Wilde's *Salome,* anticipated the Bakst style by approximately twenty years. Nevertheless he is full of admiration for the delightful effectiveness of the designs for the Russian Ballet.

His general comments on stage design are on the whole leveled against the shortcomings of the British stage. He finds that the presentation of poetic drama usually fails for lack of intensity or concentration, taste and imagination. This is to a large extent the result of division of labor,

> the instinctive mistrust of all masterful, responsible and governing minds ... which reflects the inharmonious co-operation of many men and many conflicting interests.[41]

In such a context men of the theatre often fall back upon the notion of simplicity. Ricketts would argue that "A beautiful setting should 'seem' simple when that is the character demanded by the play, not otherwise."[42] Such "seeming" simplicity is to be discovered in the inventive use of curtains. In this respect Ricketts finds Max Reinhardt's practice excellent, Craig's "mere box-like form" unimaginative. He goes on to suggest various new ways in which curtains might be used, such as a circular colonnade, open vistas, labyrinths. If he has any general principles to offer it is the

> imaginative emphasis in the preliminary choice of scenic conditions. If "a part is often better than the whole," it is certainly so in scenery; a staircase alone may suggest more of the majesty of a building than an entire palace.[43]

But he cautions that there is "no general panacea which is adequate to meet all contingencies, but many conditions which vary in their value," just as there are many different forms of drama itself.[44]

Ricketts uses the essay to highlight the inadequacies of present conditions of the British stage. He particularly objects to the "ludicrously shallow" stage, to the presence of "sky borders," to fixed proscenia, which could, with a little engineering, be made to expand and contract to suit the scale of each setting, to the complete lack of control in lighting, and especially to spurious "lighting effects" by the "thirty-shillings-a-week" limelight-man. Above all, Ricketts detects the "need of a willing and responsive audience and Press, such as a football match is able to secure."[45] He ends on the optimistic note that, while ten years ago there was no such audience in Moscow, it exists today, so that it might also exist in Britain, given time.[46]

I have endeavored in this introduction to give some indication of Ricketts' aesthetic preconceptions and of his personality. Let us now turn to an examination of the individual productions which Ricketts designed.

2

Salome (1906)

Salome was not the first production Ricketts designed. It is probable that he designed Laurence Binyon's *Paris and Oenone* in March 1906, and certain that he designed T. Sturge Moore's *Aphrodite against Artemis* a month later for the Literary Theatre Club at the King's Hall, Covent Garden.[1] The King's Hall was better known as the venue of boxing matches, but, for reasons of economy, it seems to have become a favorite location for the presentations of the various fringe theatre groups.[2] Thus when Ricketts began to design Oscar Wilde's *Salome* and *A Florentine Tragedy* for the Literary Theatre Society production in June 1906, he was already familiar with the King's Hall.

This was not the first production of the play. In Wilde's lifetime there had been talk of a production with Sarah Bernhardt, and in England J. T. Grein had planned a production in 1904 with the hope of using designs by Edward Gordon Craig. Both these planned productions came to naught, though Lugné-Poe had produced the play in 1896 in Paris to considerable critical success, and in London there was a production in 1905 at the Bijou Theatre which attracted little attention and scant praise.[3]

The Literary Theatre Society production represented for Ricketts the culmination of years of discussion and preparation.[4] We learn from *Pages on Art* that Wilde and Ricketts had studied the text with an eye to its stage presentation long before Wilde's disgrace and the Censor's banning of the play.[5] Something of their mutual respect and excitement is conveyed in the following account:

> I [Ricketts] proposed a black floor—upon which Salome's white feet, would show.... The sky was to be a rich turquoise blue, cut across by the perpendicular fall of strips of gilt matting which should not touch the ground, and so form a sort of aerial tent above the terrace.... The Jews should be in yellow, the Romans in purple, the soldiery in bronze green, and John in white. Over the dress of Salome the discussions were endless: should she be in black "like the night"? silver "like the moon"? or—here the suggestion is Wilde's—"green like a curious poisonous lizard"? I desired that the moonlight should fall upon the ground, the source not being seen; Wilde himself hugged the idea of some "strange dim pattern in the sky."[6]

This project was never realized with Wilde, of course, but Ricketts took up many of his old ideas when he finally did design the play.

A footnote in *Self-Portrait* indicates that Ricketts paid for this, and indeed other productions of the Literary Theatre Society, from the proceeds of the Vale Press edition of Marlowe's *Faustus*.[7] And it is obvious from Ricketts' diaries that he took more than a designer's share in the responsibility for this production. On March 22 we find him writing to the popular actor Henry Ainley, explaining the system whereby the literary theatre groups tended to pay nominal fees to well-known actors who might wish to take parts, and asking Ainley if he might consider the role of John the Baptist.[8] This shows that Ricketts was very familiar with the procedures of the other fringe theatre groups and that he took upon himself the role of what we should now call producer. It was a position for which he was temperamentally unsuited, though he later learned greater patience in dealing with actors. For example, when Ainley at first accepted and later withdrew, Ricketts' immediate reaction was to attribute this to the presence of a certain Mrs. Bishop in the group. It seems much more likely, however, that Ainley and other well-known actors, such as Mrs. Patrick Campbell, declined Ricketts' offer of parts in the production because of the very poor reception of the Society's first production, Sturge Moore's *Aphrodite against Artemis,* or because of other engagements.

Nor was Ricketts an ideal person to deal with the personality conflicts of a diverse group of actors. The company was made up of both professional, relatively avant-garde, actors, such as Florence Farr, Letitia Darragh and Lewis Casson, and amateur actors drawn from the literati of the day, always a volatile combination. To add to Ricketts' problems, the troublesome Mrs. Gwendoline Bishop was also responsible for the execution of his designs for the jewelry and metalwork of the production.

During the period when he was designing *Salome,* Ricketts went frequently to other theatrical presentations, *Measure for Measure* and Stephen Phillips' *Nero* on two occasions each, *Die Walküre, Captain Brassbound's Conversion,* and a new play by Barrie.[9] Ricketts' comments on *Nero* are interesting, in view of his own work at the time:

> S. Phillips has a sense of the stage. In a fine period with a living literary method he would do good work or work which would seem good.

Six days later Ricketts added:

> The play does not stand a second hearing, the vulgarity and sentimentality increase, or rather one is conscious that nothing has been done without the preoccupation of its effect upon the public.[10]

Reading between the lines, one can imagine Ricketts calculating how to avoid flashy, vulgar effects and how to draw his quarrelsome company into a fine, literary unity of purpose in their presentation.

Little is known of the work of this club or any of the other literary theatre clubs. No one person seems to have performed the duties we would now ascribe to a director. In the commercial theatres at this period rehearsals were often run through by the stage manager, or, in the case of the actor-managers, the principal actor would instruct the others as to their relative positions, business and cues. With a practiced troupe, often performing stock dramatic situations and stereotyped characters, this seemingly casual system probably worked rather smoothly.[11] The literary theatre groups were, however, presenting an entirely different type of play, often with young and inexperienced actors along with a few leading actors lending their very limited free time out of genuine interest in the development of drama. The need for a controlling artistic direction in such cases is obvious. Given the fondness of the new theatre groups for relatively obscure works, such as the plays of Maeterlinck, there also would be a need for someone simply to explain the meaning of each new work to be performed. It is not surprising, therefore, to find that Ricketts also took on the job of director, running the rehearsals for both *A Florentine Tragedy* and *Salome.*

Many would consider this an ideal situation for a new designer because he can control the whole production. Indeed it was the kind of artistic control demanded by Craig. But when we consider that Ricketts was also doing what we would call production management—running around the city trying to locate individual specialists, comparing estimates, finding appropriate materials, hiring and firing, besides much of the actual execution of the designs—one can readily understand that he was trying to do too much himself, a common failure of inexperienced directors. The cumulative effect expresses itself in frustration:

> All these black days have been spent in a rush of fussy work...intolerable delays and mistakes in matters of importance. None of my suggestions are taken with readiness or sympathy at the rehearsals. I dislike our stage-manager Jarman, I am working day and night to see things through.[12]

He was also saddled with the burden of the double-bill, two plays representing quite different historical periods. Little evidence of any kind remains concerning the production of *A Florentine Tragedy*, which may suggest Ricketts put most of his efforts into the other play.[13]

Besides the actual drawings, Ricketts seems to have stenciled the patterns onto the various dress fabrics himself, though he did use a professional stencil-cutter to cut the patterns. Stenciling was to become a favorite method in Ricketts' designs, especially when working on low-budget productions. By this means he achieved a richness and suggestiveness from relatively cheap materials. His journal indicates that he spent the afternoon of the performance nailing up the scenery, which for the most part consisted of a moonlit sky backdrop and massed clumps of drapery somewhat in the style of Appia's experimental models.[14] A glance at the design is enough to tell one that this was no lightweight set to mount. Furthermore, it gives some idea of Ricketts' practical abilities and vitiates the notion that he was merely a precious aesthete.

The production met with considerable success among the London theatre world, though the occasion was marred by a boycott by most of the press and especially by photographic journals such as *The Sketch*. The papers were still nervous about how to treat Wilde's tragedy, even though the man himself was dead. Though obviously pleased by the audience's response, Ricketts remained critical:

> Three calls at the end of *A Florentine Tragedy*, four at the end of *Salome*. Herod almost collapsed after the curtain was down. Dance begun too soon, over too soon. Salome missed covering the head of St. John with veil.[15]

The Michael Field papers give an account of the distinguished audience, and an appreciative description:

> Hardy, all of little London, George Moore, Beerbohm, Symons, Selwyn Image, Dr. Todhunter, B. Shaw, Zangwell, Yeats, Bobbie Trevelyan.... The curtain up!—At once what we came for. Eastern luxury in moonlight. A picture painted by Titian or Delacroix...no, only by Ricketts himself. Never has a stage been so wonderfully used—the picture painted by a great painter, with all the masses, lights, sparkle, glow, atmosphere of a masterpiece to set the human passion it symbolises. All the actors stand and keep their position long, giving their speeches as chords in the *Moonlight Sonata*. The whole play is full of harmony and "leit motifs", of evocations, and all this character is brought out by gesture and timbre of voice. The Herod is a most Flaubertian study, but so individualised that it is out of the tone of the music that Oscar weaves dramatically. It is somewhat too clever; but consistent and engrossing, as the sombre eyes grow hollow and the wanton mouth grows slack under the reddest red of the rose-crown. In the red of this rose-crown the highest note of the scarcely emerging, yet basal blood-red of the picture is struck for us—the red that couches in the shadow of the precious blue of the moon.
>   The other characters are in the tone of the imaginative rhetoric by which the play reaches us. Salome is a pale, exacting virgin—thirsty for tragedy.[16]

Beneath the heady praise, one catches a glimpse of the still, adamantine, tragic style of acting made famous by the Abbey Players, a style with which Ricketts, Florence Farr and Letitia Darragh, at least, would have been familiar at this date.[17] In fairness to the Michael Fields, their gushing recollection is borne out by the more disciplined appraisal of Max Beerbohm in a long and careful article, reprinted in *Last Theatres:*

> As the scenery and the dresses were designed by Mr. Charles Ricketts, it need not be said that they were beautiful. They were also, however, dramatically appropriate—just enough conventionalised to be in harmony with the peculiar character of the play. The stage-

management was faulty only in the final scene; and that, alas, is the scene where perfection is most needed. Not even that quality of Miss Darragh's acting could wholly purge our physical disgust. It is obvious that Salome ought to be in the far background, and in deepest shadow, while she holds in her hands the head of the prophet. It would aid illusion. When we distinctly see the head, we are conscious of its unreality, however realistically it be made. And our consciousness of its unreality does not make it one whit the less unpleasant.[18]

Ricketts was aware of the problem of the severed head as his statement about the misuse of the veil, quoted earlier, indicates. He quite possibly had heard of Lugné-Poe's experience in the Paris production when a wax head, specially borrowed for the occasion from Le Musée Grévin, fell off the shield and smashed to pieces.[19] Ricketts' diaries show that he spent some time rehearsing this part of the play. Wilde's text does not call for covering the head with a veil. Ricketts seems to have hit upon this solution to the problem of illusion pinpointed by Beerbohm. It is a rather clumsy method, as the poor actress would be required to manage the head, the shield (or charger) on which it sits, and a veil, while carrying on quite a bit of business with the head. The fact that no more than twenty days elapsed between the first rehearsal and the opening performance, together with the considerable production problems recorded in Ricketts' diary, would indicate that the actress simply did not have enough time to experiment and change the order or location of her acting this scene. The cast list suggests that the actors were chosen for their beauty and their powers of elocution rather than for their dexterity with stage properties. Indeed most of the play up till the severed head action falls into the pattern of slow, rhythmic rather stationary delivery with which Miss Darragh would have been familiar from her experience in Yeatsian drama.[20] The fact that *Salome* builds to a sudden burst of gruesome activity towards the end would require that the actors be well-rehearsed in this transition of tempo. Undoubtedly Ricketts was at fault in this particular case.

It is unlikely that Ricketts would ever have hit upon the solution suggested by Beerbohm, even with more rehearsal time. The different versions of the set design are all alike in that they set the cistern quite far downstage right. Three versions of the design for the stage setting exist: a photograph of an early rough sketch probably in pen and ink, in the Witt Collection of the Courtauld Institute, London, labeled "Stage Design for *Salome* 1896," which forms part of a collection of photographs and cuttings presented to the Witt Library from the Sturge Moore papers; figure 1, a finished version of the same setting, a pencil drawing which follows the main outline of the rough sketch, in the Department of Prints and Drawings at the Victoria and Albert Museum; a colored wash drawing with figures, very similar to the pencil drawing of figure 1 but showing a more elaborate setting, using the same floor plan but with several levels. This third design is in the Fitzwilliam Museum, Cambridge. There is a penciled note—the tiny handwriting is probably Ricketts'—"The Shōchiku Co., Tokyo." The figures can be identified by costume as those in figures 1 and 7.

Figure 1. *Salome*: Setting

This last set design refers to a group of designs Ricketts drew for what he refers to as a reconstruction of *Salome.*[21] In 1919, the Shōchiku Company of Tokyo requested Ricketts to design *Salome* as part of a season of European plays to be performed in Japan. Gordon Bottomley was familiar with these designs and, shortly after Ricketts' death, wrote an article for *Theatre Arts Monthly* in which he described them in great detail. Bottomley assumes the designs were lost:

> These designs never reached Japan: they went to New York on the way there, and are said to have been lost in the New York Customs.[22]

Unknown to Bottomley, the designs must have found their way back to England, or Ricketts may have retained copies of them, because this setting and several of the costume designs are clearly intended for this production. Nevertheless I feel justified in considering all of the existing drawings as a whole, with the general caveat that the designs for the later Japanese production are clearly more elaborate and more colorful. Given the evidence of continuity between the stage settings, together with Ricketts' own description of the third design as "reconstructing Salome," I shall consider all of the *Salome* material as being one example of his design.

Let us compare the different settings against the demands of the text:

> *SCENE: A great terrace in the Palace of Herod, set above the banqueting-hall. Some soldiers are leaning over the balcony. To the right there is a gigantic staircase, to the left, at the back, an old cistern surrounded by a wall of green bronze. Moonlight....* —[p. 552]
>
> *The prophet comes out of the cistern....* —[p. 557]
>
> *He goes down into the cistern....* —[p. 560]
>
> *The slaves put out the torches. The stars disappear. The great black cloud crosses the moon and conceals it completely. The stage becomes quite dark.* —[p. 574][23]

Ricketts follows the demands of the script, but for the absence of the great staircase in the first version of the design. However the stairs are cleverly indicated by the sense of distance between the balcony of the terrace and backdrop of the sky. Integral to this deception in the two later drawings is the acutely descending perspective of the wall behind the cistern, and the fact that we see only the top part of the one mighty column, so that it seems to rise from a lower courtyard or hall, perhaps at the foot of a flight of descending stairs. A feeling of depth in the great terrace is achieved by the backward sloping draperies which recede from the front of the stage to some point in the far distance, appropriately left vague because obscured by the heavy massing of drapery downstage which forms a kind of private tent or enclosure for a double throne and floor cushions, intended for the royal party. This enclosure would draw the exchanges between Herod, Herodias and Salome into a very intimate grouping which could cause blocking problems, but it does create the feeling of a location with a vast palace in the background.

Ricketts' decision to place this enclosure so far downstage demands that, to be seen in relation to the rest of the actors, Salome must act her final business with the severed head right at the front of the stage. The cistern, which must be the cylindrical object on the floor, stage right, is about halfway back; another clump of drapery throws a shadow over it and partly obscures it. The actress is bound to move downstage to enable the other actors to react to her gruesome antics. Thus Beerbohm's criticism. Ricketts would be restricted, as to the placing of the cistern, by the necessity for a trap door, since the text demands that Jokanaan must rise out of, and descend into, the well.

Thirteen years later the "reconstructed" design does not offer any new solution to the problem. The stage is opened up somewhat by the fact that the central block of drapery is replaced, in terms of composition, by a great rectangular pillar rising from a raised dais which is part of a flight of stairs leading onto the terrace. There would seem to be no need for the double throne to remain so far downstage but we find it in exactly the same position as before, just as the cistern remains midway back, stage right. The flight of stairs and the various levels would make exits and entrances more effective, but the basic blocking problem remains.

There are two possible solutions, other than Beerbohm's suggestion of setting the action far back. The scene could be acted in a very pale, obscure light. It is quite possible that this was Ricketts' initial plan, as his diaries during the rehearsal period fulminate against the ineptitude of the lighting man. Yet, no matter how well this solution were executed, it would create another problem. When Herod leaves the stage he orders darkness, and with true pathetic fallacy the stars go out and the moon is obscured by clouds. If this sudden darkening is to have any effect, the immediately preceding action must be well lit. Yet another way out of the problem would be to find some excuse for Herod and his attendants to rise and move back upstage, leaving Salome a greater area in which to act out her ugly scene.

The major alteration in the Japanese setting is in the use of color: the red of the soldier's lances which had formerly been the only relief from the dominant blues and greens of the stage picture, has in the later setting been added to the three perpendicular pillars which replace the "dim cypress-like curtains against a star-lit sky" of the earlier production.[24] The later design retains the same basic composition but introduces greater variety of form, texture and color.

Of the costume designs which still exist, most seem to date from the planned Japanese production, but, as can be seen from the various written accounts, the costume designs, like the modifications of the set, represent development of the original ideas rather than a change of concept. It seems apposite to quote from three accounts of the costume designs at this stage. Ricketts describes the 1906 King's Hall production:

The players were clothed in every shade of blue, deepening into dark violet and green, the general harmony of blue on blue relieved by the red lances of the soldiers,[25]

and Robert Ross takes up the theme:

Salome dressed in a mist rising by moonlight with a train of blue and black moths. Herodias in a peacock train of dahlias and a horned tiara. Herod is robed in silver and blue lined with flame decorated with griffons, sphynxes and angels,[26]

and Bottomley, remembering the designs he had seen, years before, for the Japanese production:

This set of designs, showed his stage-work at its most fortunate heights: the costumes were in a vein of passionate fantasy mingled with a use of decoration deliciously contrived to appeal to the country of Ukio-ye, Herodias wearing a robe of black and yellow that suggested not only a tigress but a tigress "burning bright" with searing flame, Herod's rich apparel and black beard and hair being given a sinister touch of unfathomed depravity by a coronal of innocent pink roses in his hair, the Jews' large patterned dresses, beards and pointed high caps marking them off sharply from the Romans: the scene a fragment of a high colonnade against a dark luminous night.[27]

Many of the designs left by Ricketts, now in the National Arts-Collection Fund, have never been identified as belonging to particular productions; therefore one is often left to make an educated guess based on a reading of the various plays Ricketts designed. Of the eight designs which I am assuming to be intended for either production of *Salome,* the designs for Romans, Jews (fig. 6) and a Negro (fig. 4) appear to date from the earlier period. Two soldiers and a slave (fig. 2), young Syrian (fig. 3), Herod (fig. 8), Herodias (fig. 7), and Salome (fig. 5) can be assumed to date from the later period.[28] Because of the slightly oriental features it is relatively easy to separate these two groups of costume designs. Ricketts' style also changed considerably in the thirteen years which separate the two groups. The earlier designs use a freer hand to represent robust, rounded figures. The later group of designs demonstrates greater concern for presentation, for the design as a finished drawing worthy of framing. The figures are invariably elongated, astringent, muscular, with flesh drawn tightly over prominent bone structures, usually with the hollow cheeks and deep-set eyes of Ricketts' high style. If, as seems likely, this second group is based upon a live model, he must surely be the same model whose familiar features haunt some of Ricketts' easel paintings such as *Don Juan.*[29] Despite the differences in rendering of the two groups, and the lapse of years between, the two sets of costumes would happily marry into one production, and it is clear that, for both productions, the designer carefully orchestrated his use of color and pattern with a concern for dramatic rhythm and the movement of groups of figures about the stage.

The play opens with the soldiers, the young Syrian and the page of Herodias looking down from the terrace into the courtyard or banquet hall below. No sketch for the page has survived, but one for the young Syrian (fig. 3) and a design for two soldiers and a slave (fig. 2) are enough to tell us how Ricketts planned his first stage picture in this dim, moonlit setting. Predominantly black with touches of color in the stenciled patterns, exotic headgear, considerable areas of exposed flesh, heavy shields and willowy red lances—the scene cries out for silhouette lighting against a distant star—splashed indigo backdrop representing the night sky.

Also on stage, but obscurely lit, is the huge Negro executioner to whom the first group of young men refer. Perhaps he crouches in the shadow of the upright columns, somewhere close to the cistern-prison which he guards. As the young men refer to him he may move his head slightly and the first glint of his gold earring is picked up in the light which slowly spills over his oiled arm and his white tunic.

Next on stage is Salome herself. But for those descriptions quoted above, we know little of the colors she wears; all that has come down to us is a pencil drawing, possibly a tracing, pasted into a folio of rough sketches for several productions.[30] In contrast to the busy, scintillating figure of Salome stands the patient bowed figure of the green-clad slave sent to summon the princess back to Herod (fig. 2).

No illustration exists of Jokanaan, but the text leads us to expect a simple, white tunic, chaste but open a little at the neck, to make sense of Salome's lines about his white flesh. Jokanaan returns to the cistern and the stage picture seems empty till the magnificent entry of the court, Herod, Herodias and attendants who proceed downstage in a great sweep of color. The attendant figures from many nations probably group downstage right, providing a mass of color, of pattern upon pattern, each group identified by one strong color and by individually shaped headgear. The focal point is the double throne, whereon sit Herod and his queen dressed in robes of black with touches of blue, green, gold, silver, flame and violet. Now that the stage is set, there will be some movement, particularly from Salome, but the basic groupings of color and mass remain until Herod and the court exit and the stage darkens, while the heavy shields clash inwards on the frail, petulant figure of Salome, and the curtain drops. This account of the movement and rhythm of color and pattern, though hypothetical, is based upon the evidence of the setting and a careful reading of the text. Let us now examine the individual costume designs more closely.

The drawing of soldiers and slave (fig. 2) shows three different costumes. The slave wears a long tunic of green stuff with patches of blue and braids of white decorated with tiny black chevrons. The braids are both decorative and functional as they serve to cover and reinforce the seams. A heavy Egyptian hairstyle is bound with a simple white strip of cloth, and the white is repeated in

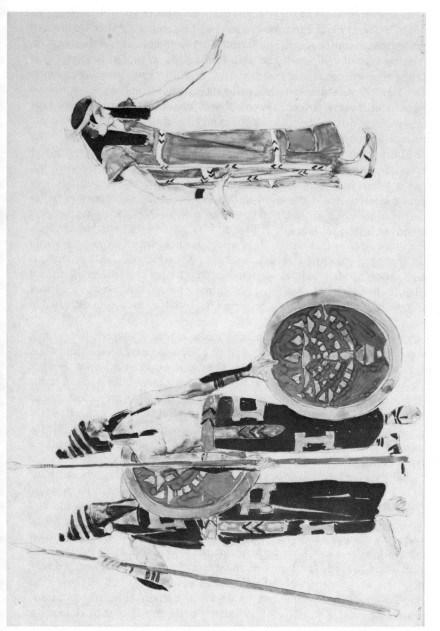

Figure 2.   *Salome*: Soldiers and Slave
            (Courtesy Victoria and Albert Museum)

a heavy, round, pendant earring. A contrasting touch of color is provided by the simple red and black shoes with turned-up toes. If nothing else told us, the cowed, suppliant stance of this figure would indicate that this is a slave sent on the fruitless task of calling Salome back to the banquet below. It is typical of Ricketts that, by depicting the huddled posture of this figure standing patiently waiting, he creates a still green point in the stage composition, while the frenetic figure of Salome moves about in her diaphanous costume trying to provoke the benign figure of Jokanaan. The suppliant green and the proud, defiant white figure of Jokanaan would contrast vividly with the glittering princess in her myriad hues, strutting obsessively about the darkened stage. From a study of the costumes we perceive not only the achievement of Ricketts the designer, but also something of Ricketts the director with his concern for composition, rhythm and even characterization in the way he renders the posture of his figures. To many a designer the minor role of the slave might seem unimportant, a last-minute job of rags and scraps, but Ricketts has carefully dressed the character in a plain, rather severe garment which looks natural and gentle against the tortured wreaths and garlands which decorate Salome. If further proof of this pointed contrast were needed it is to be found in comparing the two hairstyles: the slave is almost bowed down under the black luxuriance of her abundant hair; Salome's hair is either hidden or distorted in its close-fitting treatment.

In the same design (fig. 2) stand two soldiers, very similar to one another, yet just different enough to provide interest. The costume is black with a square pattern of gold, an ankle-length tubular skirt which may or may not be worn with a simple square top, buckled at the shoulders. One soldier is naked to the waist, the chest of the other is covered. Both wear long grey cloth sashes decorated with black chevrons. The pattern is carefully worked out, so that the soldier without the top is compensated with black-thonged sandals, while the other goes barefoot. Similarly the half-naked soldier has a pattern of three chevrons on the pendant of his sash, while the other has two. These details seem slight, but they are an important indication of how a designer can establish the mood of a play. Here the seeming casualness, the little personal differences, do not indicate rank, as chevrons would, for example, in a contemporary military costume (otherwise the soldier with the sandals and the three chevrons would undoubtedly be more heavily-attired, less naked, than his companion), rather they show that the soldiers are domestic guards in a household where discipline is slack, where the order of things might be overturned at any moment. I do not propose that the members of the audience consciously worked all these hints out; nevertheless the anticipations set up are altogether different from those that would be created by a line of completely uniform palace guards. In other aspects of attire, the dressing of beards and hair, helmets, arm-greaves, shields and spears, the two soldiers are identical. The leatherwork of sandals and greaves is typical of the style Ricketts used throughout his design career. The upward sweep of the gold and black helmets and the large gold earrings making hair, beard and helmet seem almost of one piece, elongate Ricketts' attenuated figures even more, giving an impression of great height which is continued by the tapering red lances with their gilt spearheads. In the massive shields with their stenciled gold-on-blue, slightly Hebraic, pattern Ricketts' great concern for props is demonstrated. The gold design echoes the gold of the costumes and helmets, but, to give them the prominence they need for their final horrible purpose, their base color is not the same black of the costumes, nor even the dull grey of the sashes, but a deep, relentless blue. And, of course, they appear heavy enough, and are big enough, to make the final crushing of Salome realistic, while providing a crouched actress with sufficient room to hide convincingly.

The young Syrian (fig. 3) who shall take his own life, tormented by Salome's momentary adoration of Jokanaan, wears a costume which, like that of the soldiers with whom he first appears on stage, is black relieved by touches of color and pattern. The solid, white geometrical design on the skirt is cleverly reversed on the top to form white shoulder straps and a yoke. The costume is basically two overlapping aprons, one at the back the other at the front, held together by white shoulder straps and by a long deep green scarf bound twice around the waist, forming a convenient sword belt. The severity of the costume is relieved by the flowing lines of the waistband and by a blue fringe around the hem. The green of the waistband is taken up in the long flowing material which forms part of the headdress. This veil is decorated with a small black pattern. The rest of the headdress consists of a blue conical hat with long panels which suspend from behind the ears and extend over the shoulders, the whole bound around the temples with a deep band of gold, surmounted by a long, backward-sloping blue feather. The bare arms are decorated with gold, black, blue and white armbands. The feet are clad in red and black shoes with upward-pointed, rather oriental toes, typical of Ricketts' shoe designs. The red and black of the shoes is repeated in the decoration of the sword sheath. The point of the overlapping apron style of the dress becomes obvious when one thinks about the sword. The back and front sections are lashed together by black straps at the armpit, thus leaving a deep, naked V-shaped area of flesh from armpit to waist. This would form a natural target for the entry of the fatal knife, and also provide a convincing means of faking the deathblow without the necessity of slashing the costume and fiddling with simulated blood. We are told later that there is blood upon the floor, but this might be done by a number of means other than seeming to pour from the young man's chest. The costume is a careful combination of hard and soft features; the tight armbands and hard-edged patterns are softened by the flowing scarves, the deep fringe, the delicate sandals. Here is a young boy of gentle birth, dressed with all the care we expect from one who "had much joy to gaze at himself in the river," struggling with his first adult infatuation for the remote, unscrupulous beauty of Salome.

Figure 3.   *Salome*: Young Syrian
            (Courtesy Victoria and Albert Museum)

Unfortunately no design for his bosom companion, the page of Herodias, has survived but it seems probable that he would have appeared, as part of the first stage picture, predominantly in black. To complement the costumes of the soldiers and the young Syrian, the page's uniform might well have echoed the yellow or violet which contribute to the dress of his mistress, Herodias.

The design for the Negro (fig. 4) may represent the executioner from *Salome*, though it has simply been labeled "unidentified negro" and could belong to a number of productions Ricketts designed. The Negro appears to have been drawn in the same manner as the Romans (in the Usher Art Gallery, Lincoln) and the Jews (fig. 6) and to be costumed in fabric with a similar type of large-scale stenciled decoration. He is tall, barefoot, muscular as would befit the part of executioner in this play, and his long, bare arm would look impressive thrust forth from the cistern with the severed head on a silver charger. His short, wide tunic hangs from one shoulder strap, and is bound at the top by a strip of solid brown; a streamer of this material also falls down the front of the costume, mingling with the crushed white sash which secures the tunic at the waist. He wears a tight-fitting brown cap with a pointed crown reminiscent of those on the famous Benin bronzes of Nigeria.[31] He also wears a tight white or silver bracelet, and a huge crescent-shaped gold earing, similar to the pendant decorations on Herodias' headdress. He moves with a lazy grace and self-confidence, as if his bloody office were somehow beneath his notice, something done automatically and upon command.

Into this picture of blues, blacks and greens, with little touches of white, brown and red, strides Salome. We have little more than an outline drawing (fig. 5) and various descriptions of her costume. The discussions of Ricketts and Wilde suggest the costume might be black or silver or a poisonous green.[32] The diary entry for 25 May 1906 tells us that Ricketts bought an "admirable silver tissue threaded with black and with red" for Salome's dress.[33] Robbie Ross has described "Salome dressed in a mist rising by moonlight, with a train of blue and black moths."[34] None of these descriptions is very definite and the drawing is the best guide. It shows a sensuous costume, daring for its day, providing enough opportunity for both color and modesty in the masses of flowers which decorate the waist and free-flowing arm panels. The head is a close-fitting cap of overlapping discs, possibly more flowers, or tightly curled hair, or spangles, or a combination of all of these, which continues down into a long, heavy braid swinging freely to about the waist. It seems reasonable to assume from the various descriptions that the costume was basically silver-grey with touches of black, blue and possibly red. The legs are fully covered in harem-type pants caught tightly at the ankles and bound with drapery and garlands at the waist. In construction it is not unlike Ricketts' costume for Lillah McCarthy in Arnold Bennett's *Judith* (see pp. 99-102), in that the very low waistline would be impossible to keep up but for the bands of material which join the bust section to the hip garland. Naturally this means that the top has to

Figure 4.   [*Salome*: Executioner]
(*Courtesy Ashmolean Museum, Oxford*)

Figure 5.   [*Salome*: Salome]
              (Courtesy Victoria and Albert Museum)

be bound very tightly if, as in the drawing, there is no support strap round the neck or shoulders. However uncomfortable it may be for the actress to wear, it certainly makes the suicide of the young Syrian and the weak groveling of Herod seem believable, and that, after all, should be the first concern of both actress and designer. In the sketch she is barefoot, but we know from the text that she takes sandals off on stage. Therefore the drawing shows Salome at her most naked.

Of the various ethnic groups of characters which surround the tetrarch Herod and his queen, only designs for the Romans and the Jews remain, both designs showing a pair of figures. The style of presentation suggests that these date from the 1906 production. The rendering of the figures in pairs suggests that Ricketts intended the various nationalities to be seen in groups, superimposed one upon the other, as they surround the central action of the play.

The design for the Romans suggests the flush vulgarity of an empire already on the brink of decline. The men's bare heads are proud but heavy-featured, almost stupid. The purple costumes are decorated with huge motifs. Tassels sweep the ground.

By contrast the design for the Jews (fig. 6) shows two figures wearing black and white apronlike robes with long yellow scarves and yellow pants. Their solemn dignity sets them apart from the Romans. Their robes are fringed in a dull, steel blue. As usual, Ricketts takes great care to characterize the roles, in the dressing of the hair and beards, in the provision of appropriate props such as the blue and white walking stick and the tambourine, and by the distinctive headdresses. The Jews wear high white caps, like rounded cones with little touches of red trim. Long white streamers fall down in front of the shoulders.

While the various embassies and courtiers take up their positions around the stage, Herod and his queen proceed to the double throne. Herodias (fig. 7) wears a long, fishtail train of black, splashed with irregular diamond-shaped patches of yellow, each with a deeper touch of brown-gold at its center like the half-shut eye of a cat. The robe is lined with gold. Underneath the train she wears a soft tunic of violet which repeats the same gold and brown diamond-shaped pattern of the cloak. Her waist is loosely bound with a long green sash. She wears elevated, platform shoes of gold and red, and she carries the gilt palm-shaped fan she demands from her page. As is often the case, Ricketts is most imaginative in the headdress. A tall golden helmet, which completely encases the head, brims upwards from Herodias' painted face to a smooth, flat crown. At the front it is decorated with touches of blue and a pair of dangling, crescent-shaped pieces reminiscent of the cruel moon so often referred to in the text and of the similarly shaped earring of the executioner. At the front of the helmet is draped a soft blue scarf which completely conceals the ears and neck, exposing only a hint of black-red, henna-dyed hair. From the back of the helmet, just above the neck, springs a great folded golden arch which repeats

Figure 6.   *Salome*: Jewish Priests
            (Courtesy Victoria and Albert Museum)

Figure 7.   *Salome:* Herodias
(*Courtesy Victoria and Albert Museum*)

the shape of the horned crescents dangling at the front. A back view of the costume reveals that this folded, arched section is held in place by a massive, diagonally placed, gold pin to which are attached four veils: the blue chin scarf, a long thin green ribbon of the same fabric as the sash at her waist, a mass of silky flame material bunched across the shoulders and hanging to the floor, and finally at the center back a scarf of yellow and black of greater intensity than the black and gold robe against which it hangs. The headdress itself is magnificent; crowning the rest of the costume, it is the summation of Herodias' vanity and malignity. As Bottomley points out, the costume with its great train suggests the tigress which would have been especially appealing to the Japanese. Indeed the drawing recalls the feline grace of certain Kabuki characters.

Herodias' costume is doubly impressive in relation to the costumes of the other characters. Consider Salome's costume. The princess's ability to control the course of events increases as she gradually undresses. Herodias' power over Herod decreases throughout the play and her obvious care to conceal her aging charms in the outward trappings of power becomes an ironic comment upon her ineffectuality. Herodias always appears in conjunction with Herod (fig. 8). The two costumes viewed together would have been spectacular. And now one sees Ricketts' purpose in granting the double throne such a prominent situation. Impressive as these two figures would seem as they sweep downstage together, it would take a moment for their full effect to be realized. With the characters standing or seated together the combination of color, mass and outline would be cohesive, yet the two costumes characterize the two figures precisely. Herodias' costume with its sweeping train, its semicircular sleeves, its scintillating, irregular pattern, its massive headdress is prop to a vanity already quite unsure of itself. Herod, who at first sight seems to be almost as overwhelmed by his costume as his queen by hers, is in fact all too naked; his costume provides an inadequate shelter behind which to conceal his weakness.

The key to the difference in costume is the neck. The queen's neck could not be more hidden. Herod's neck is bare, white, vulnerable—despite his tugging hand adjusting the great weight of his cloak. Unlike the queen's, Herod's cloak is cut on the square, given form by the primitive method of bunching it together at the shoulders into two massive golden brooches. It is not for nothing that he holds the neck cords, since the drag of such a weight concentrated on the shoulders could very easily choke him. The heavy gold earrings and the dark mass of hair complete the downwards thrust of the outline of the cloak. The feeling of weight is increased by the deep pink of the lining which hugs the floor, and by the immensity of the silver and gold pattern on the blue outer layer of the robe. Because it drags on the floor this cloak would be much less manageable than the great sea-cloak Ricketts was to design later for Cuchulain in the Yeats plays. Cuchulain's cloak is designed to protect and elevate, while Herod's exposes and subjugates. Herod is bogged down by this symbol of his office and he is powerless to alter this situation. Ironically the

Figure 8. [*Salome*: Herod]
(*Courtesy Tate Gallery*)

design shows him holding onto the cloak with one hand, while lifting a drinking vessel in the other. The undergarment is a long black tunic overlaid with a windowpane or net design, and a center panel of gold and blue. The deep hem is decorated with large octagonal patterns. The sleeve is of the same material as the hem. The shoes of black and dull red repeat the red of the rose crown. The huge black death ring glistens on a pallid, white hand. As Herod slips the ring from his finger, in final submission to Salome's will, he drops his head into the folds of his great cloak.

Taken as a whole the designs give some idea of the excitement felt by the first audience. The designs are striking in their radical use of a simplified historical approach. No stage-designer of the period was a greater expert on the arts and decoration of the ancient Near East. Yet in his designs, Ricketts eschews a painstaking historical accuracy, and he does so deliberately. Wilde's *Salome* was not a museum tableau for Ricketts, but a tragic drama expressing poetic rather than archaeological truths. In this, one of the earliest productions he designed, he displays the direction so much of his later stage work was to take; while evoking a specific, historic period he avoids an unimaginative realism and achieves a simplified artistic intensity through the careful manipulation of the designer's basic resources, light, mass, shape and color. In a private letter the art critic Roger Fry gives some idea of the effect of the 1906 production upon informed, artistic opinion:

> We've just been to see Oscar Wilde's *Salome* superbly mounted and acted and it really came out something altogether greater than one had any idea of. Herod became a quite Shakespearian conception. C. Ricketts did the staging with ideas of colour that surpassed belief. I've never seen anything so beautiful on the stage.[35]

3

The Death of Tintagiles (1912)

Between 1906 and 1912 Ricketts continued to design for the theatre, most notably the 1907 production of Binyon's *Attila* at His Majesty's and a 1909 *King Lear* at the Haymarket Theatre. He maintained his interest in designing for the new poetic drama of the little theatres but also worked for the larger, west-end managements. Ricketts' work of this period is best characterized by an exploratory sense of color symbolism in his designs, his all red scene in *Attila* having been particularly remarkable. The next production I wish to discuss in detail is Maeterlinck's *The Death of Tintagiles*. This short play is never likely to have enjoyed a long run, yet it had a strange vogue for a time, and this particular production is mentioned years later by those who saw it.

The original French publication of the play dates from 1894. The play was dedicated to A.F. Lugné-Poe. It was first published in English in the journal *The Pageant* in 1896. Gide records a production in Paris at Le Théâtre des Maturins in 1906 and C.B. Purdom mentions a Stage Society production at the Globe Theatre, London, on 29 April 1900 in a program with Maeterlinck's *Interior* and Fiona MacLeod's *The House Of Usna*.[1] The production which Ricketts designed opened 17 December 1912 at the St. James's and was revived in 1913 at the Savoy. It played together with Galsworthy's *The Silver Box* and was produced by Harley Granville Barker.[2]

The years 1907 and 1914 are not covered by the manuscript journals in the Ricketts papers at the British Library, but letters indicate that during December 1912 he was traveling in Egypt. The design work for this production must have been completed before his departure. He did see the revival in 1913 because he later refers to this, along with a 1914 production of Masefield's *Philip the King* at Covent Garden, as one of the two plays he ever designed which he considered to have been successfully lit.[3]

The original publication in 1894 had described *The Death of Tintagiles* and its two companion plays, *Alladine and Palomides* and *Interior*, as marionette plays. Maeterlinck's theoretical writings on the subject of puppet drama are well known, but, as with all his writings, the reader must consider the often extreme fluctuations of theory in relation to the events of Maeterlinck's personal life.[4] Certainly by the 1900s his idea about puppets as preferable to actors had been modified as a result of his association with the actress Georgette Leblanc. The 1906 Paris production already referred to was a star vehicle with Leblanc playing Ygraine before an audience which included such famous theatrical ladies as Mary Garden and Eleanora Duse. Maeterlinck himself was in the house, which would indicate that he no longer regarded flesh and blood actors as an unnecessary hindrance to the creation of his peculiarly atmospheric dramas.[5] This play's brief popularity, relative to Maeterlinck's other short dramas about death, can surely be attributed to the fact that the leading female role, that of Ygraine, would have been attractive to actresses of the high poetic tradition such as Georgette Leblanc and Lillah McCarthy. Apart from such human considerations, the play's technical demands, for example, lifting up the limp body of a child, splintering a sword in a doorjamb, disentangling arms and fingers caught up in the hair of other sleeping characters, would be well nigh impossible for puppeteers to manage effectively. Certainly by the time of the 1912 production which Ricketts designed there is no evidence that anyone even considered *The Death of Tintagiles* as a puppet play.

Granville Barker and Ricketts between them probably came closer to realizing in this production Maeterlinck's ideas of character in relation to destiny than could have been achieved by the mechanical means of puppets. Ricketts' designs emphasize the characters as idealized, diminutive figures in a darkened setting, so overwhelmed by impending doom that their actions became ritualistic, lacking spontaneity. Without resorting to puppets, which are at least potentially ridiculous, Ricketts achieved an effect similar to that Maeterlinck aimed at in developing his marionette theory, portraying not the ordinary life of individual characters but the superior life of the infinite as it is revealed to the poet's sensibility.

The play is divided into five very brief sections, set in four locations, involving three changes of set: on top of a hill overlooking the castle, a room in the castle, the same, a corridor in front of the last, and before a great iron door in a gloomy vault.[6] All that remains of Ricketts' set design are three tiny working sketches in the Harvard Theatre Collection and a photograph of a rough sketch in the Witt Collection at the Courtauld Institute, London (fig. 9). These show a draped proscenium before a semicircle of dark, massed drapery with, in addition, five separate pillar-like sections. These soft columns of curtains can also reveal a fixed backdrop which is divided horizontally into light and dark sections at a level which would be some two or three feet above the head of a standing male figure. The impression is that of a high wall with the night sky beyond. Between the two central columns of drapes there is a dark section or flat with a very high semicircular grill which could indicate a prison cell, or the top of a large gate. One of the curtains is pulled and tied back in such a way that it might indicate a corridor leading off to one side. By simply rearranging these separate curtains the various locations demanded by the text

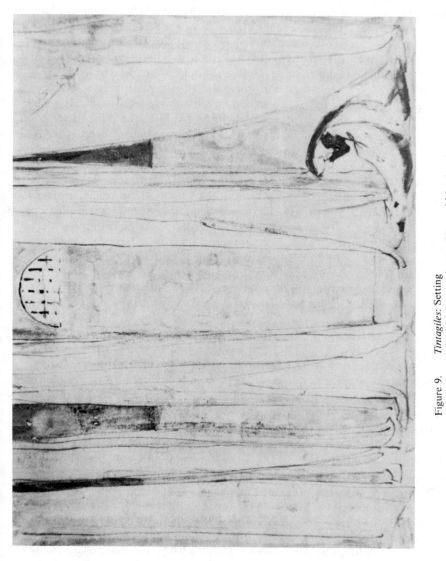

Figure 9.   *Tintagiles*: Setting
(Courtesy Witt Library, Courtauld Institute)

could be quickly established. Speed of setting each scene would be essential, as the play unfolds in an atmosphere of ever increasing darkness leading to the ultimate blackout in which Ygraine's final lines are spoken.

The sketches indicate a narrow and rather shallow acting area. This has the compensating effect of an illusion of great height which suits the demands of the play, since it establishes the vulnerability of the characters, who cannot ever see their enemy, while maintaining the possibility, the fear, that they are being overlooked from behind the wall or beyond the grill. The idea of impending doom, of mystery and insecurity, would be increased by the fact that some of the doors, chambers, corridors referred to cannot be seen. The four figures trying to resist the unknown, unseen evil would seem lost in a tiny pool of light somewhere at the center of a labyrinth. The one door at the end of Act III has to be convincingly solid, as it takes the combined strengths of Aglovale, Ygraine and Bellangère to close it, and Aglovale's sword splinters against its surrounding framework. In Act V there is yet another "great iron door" behind which Tintagiles is imprisoned. It is not a functional door but should seem solid enough to muffle the child's cries, to withstand Ygraine's repeated hammerings with clenched fists, and to make her smashing of the earthenware lamp against it seem convincing. For this last reason it would have to be more fireproof than the standard frame and painted canvas type of stage door. If the high structure with the arched grill is, indeed, the Act V "great iron door," which may well have had to be specially constructed, it would seem likely that both the St. James's and the Savoy could have supplied a stock door and heavy frame for Act III. One of the Harvard sketches gives construction details for a prisonlike door.

The play is one of Maeterlinck's symbolic treatments of love's futile struggle against death. This type of play can best be served by simple and equally symbolic treatment of light and shade. The essential feature of the set is the lighting of stage and drapery to suggest mystery and foreboding and to create a definite but diminishing pool of warmth in a vast surrounding of nebulous darkness, leading up to the final blackout. Ricketts' set design suggests that he met the demands of the text with imagination and economy.

It is interesting to compare Ricketts' design with the often reproduced version by Sapounov for the 1905 Meyerhold production at the Studio Theatre, Moscow. Sapounov's design has an early Renaissance, almost Florentine lightness of touch. It has a highly decorated, pattern upon pattern effect which Denis Bablet perceptively traces to Meyerhold's concern, at this time, for the pictorial convention of two-dimensional space, similar in style to that of Russian church icons.[7] The busy accumulation of architectural styles and pretty details could not be more different from Ricketts' design. While there is nothing that is manifestly at odds with the text, the Russian design lacks the essential uncanny expectancy which Ricketts' sketch suggests.

Several designs and photographs of the costumes exist. The Victoria and Albert Museum has one superbly finished watercolor of the three servants of the queen.[8] The Bottomley Collection donated to the Carlisle Museum and Art Gallery includes one finished design for Ygraine and Tintagiles (the design reproduced in Lillah McCarthy's *Myself and My Friends*) plus three rough sketches annotated in Ricketts' hand.

The Carlisle designs correspond closely with the production photographs Bottomley published, courtesy of Lillah McCarthy, Lady Keeble, in his obituary article on Ricketts in *Theatre Arts Monthly.*[9] The outline of the costumes is, generally speaking, early medieval. The stenciled patterns are large in area yet delicate in the way they fold into the flowing lines of the materials. The general impression is gothic, strange, with the aura of a distant antiquity unrelated to any too-specific period. The play involves a great deal of hurried movement and fairly strenuous activity, such as grasping doors, carrying a sleeping child, moving in unison with arms clasped around one another. Yet the flow of Ricketts' designs would not impede movement. He uses tight, close-fitting sleeves, concentrating the fullness of the costumes in the trains. His headdresses suggest the remote, mythic strangeness of the play, while keeping the hair well back from the face, arms and chest. As usual, great care is taken with such details as shoes, gloves and hand props.

The design for Bellangère consists of a plain undergarment of cobalt blue with the note "velvet skin-tight" and a flowing tabard or overdress in green, closely patterned in white arabesques or tear-shaped figures with black center spots, somewhat reminiscent of peacock feathers. The robe tumbles in heavy folds around the feet, which would create the sound of hushed sighs on stage and give the sense, appropriate to the play, of dragging the character down with the weight of insuperable odds. A typical Ricketts touch is the use of two belts, one delicate, high-waisted, ostensibly holding the back and front of the dress together, the other lower, heavier, seeming to pull the character downwards. From the higher belt two side panels depend. The note indicates "stenciled black on silver satin." These panels emphasize the length of the figure and seem to contain the bright riot of green, white and blue beneath. The second belt is, in fact, four separate bands sewn side by side. A note reads: "black velvet sewn with pearls. This must be very heavy and sewn onto the dress. Use silver satin for metal plaques." A black strap hangs in irregular lengths from the middle of the belt. It is typical of Ricketts that, while wishing the belt to look heavy, he has thought out the problem of the distribution of weight and given the advice that the metal buckles be replaced by lighter fabric, and the whole sewn onto the dress. The headdress is a closely fitted black cap with a broad chin strap, secured and decorated with heavy discs of a dull gold braid over each ear. Strands of this braid cross the head from ear to ear. The hair flows freely from the back of the cap. The braided discs over the ears might be the typical, medieval or Viking "earphone" hairstyle or a decoration made from metal or metallic fabric. He probably recognized that few actresses would have enough hair for both the "earphones" and the full fall of hair at the back, which the text demands. A wig or a partial wig would be a solution that might appeal to any actress wishing to keep her hair:

First Servant.	We shall not be able to open his hands.
Second Servant.	They are plunged deep into his sister's hair.
First Servant.	He holds one golden curl between his little teeth.
Second Servant.	We shall have to cut the elder sister's hair.
First Servant.	And the other sister's too, you will see.
Second Servant.	Have you your scissors?
Third Servant.	Yes. [pp. 112-13]

and, later, the stage direction

> *One of them carries Tintagiles, who is fast asleep, in her arms. From his little hands, twitching in sleep, and his mouth, drawn in agony, a glittering stream of golden tresses, ravished from the heads of his sisters, flow down to the ground.* [p. 115]

The production photograph (fig. 10) reproduced in Bottomley's article shows the actress who plays Bellangère kneeling and wearing the tight cap with metallic decoration over masses of free-flowing hair. If a wig was used the close-fitting headdress would have provided a secure and convenient anchor.

The design for Ygraine (which includes the child Tintagiles) follows a similar line to that of the costume for her sister (fig. 11). The undergarment is black with the same tight-fitting sleeves. The underskirt is fuller and larger than the overdress, extending about four inches beyond the top layer, forming a kind of black border. The white tabard has a stenciled black checkered design arranged in a half-drop repeat. The checkered pattern echoes the grill which is the dominant decorative feature of the set design. The chainlike design and the black border formed by the undergarment have the visual effect of seeming to pull the figure down, as if she is trapped by the oppressive environment. The stark black and white of the costume is relieved by a simple blue yoke at the neck. Touches of blue are repeated in the cap. A series of five silver straps closes each side of the overdress. The text calls for golden hair, but, as the whole design project sprang from the close friendship among Ricketts, Granville Barker (who directed the play) and Barker's wife, Lillah McCarthy, the sketch obviously takes Lillah's luxuriant dark hair into account. The hair is bound by a series of white fillets into one great heavy lock which hangs down from the back of the cap. The headdress is similar to that worn by Bellangère, except that it is given a slightly oriental look by the use of overlapping black triangular folds, set off with blue. The decorative disc which secures the chin strap and covers the ear is smaller, and the whole is finished with a long blue-grey scarf of a gauze fabric which hangs down behind.

Figure 10.   *Tintagiles*: Ygraine, Bellangère and Tintagiles
             (Courtesy Enthoven Collection, Victoria and Albert
             Museum)

Figure 11.   *Tintagiles*: Ygraine and Tintagiles
(Courtesy Bottomley Bequest, Carlisle)

This design includes Tintagiles. The child wears a green-blue, close-fitting shirt, and leggings with white bindings. Over these clothes he wears a sleeveless tunic with a herringbone design in brown and gold, seamed and hemmed in a black braid of a simple squared pattern. The tunic contains a large patch pocket made from a different material of a larger, floral pattern in blue and gold, outlined in the same braid as the rest of the garment. In the production photograph (fig. 10) the detailed pattern on the tunic is lost, but that on the braid stands out, suggesting that it may have been woven with metallic thread. The child's hair falls to the shoulders in a square-cut, rather pre-Raphaelite style. As if to emphasize the pathos of the child's innocence, Ricketts has included in the design a squat little wooden toy horse. In the Granville Barker production the prince, Tintagiles, was, in fact, played by a little girl.[10]

The design for what Ricketts calls "the old man humbug Aglovale" in a note on the design, shows an old man dressed in shades of pale grey and black. The principal feature of the costume is a loose grey tunic with matching cape. It has pale grey fur trim at the hem, and a hood thrown back on the shoulders. The tunic is slit to the waist and closed by a heavy black sword belt. The full, open sleeve has a gold design which Ricketts notes is "gold stenciling on one sleeve only." The legs and feet are encased in black trimmed with white or silver. Aglovale wears a long white beard and a plain black skullcap, and he carries the sword which eventually breaks in the effort to defend Tintagiles from the unseen pursuers in Act III. The costume effectively suggests both dignity and frailty, an old soldier past his best strength but trying still to protect his young charge from the unseen, malign queen. But for the cap, which pinpoints a particular period more precisely than anything else in this set of designs, the old man might be one of the mythical old kings in the Irish plays Ricketts designed for Yeats. Further notes on the design give the source and price of the material, and instructions, presumably to the dressmaker, to return the sketch: "Green and Abbot, 475 Oxford Street, 2/11 yd. 50 inches" and "please return this."

Some confusion exists concerning the costumes of the servants of the queen. Both in the French and in the English versions, the text indicates that the servants are female. The production photograph and the design from the Bottomley collection (fig. 12) show the servants as male. There also exists at the Victoria and Albert Museum a highly finished design (fig. 13), exquisitely executed as to composition and rendering, which shows the three servants as female. Normally one would hesitate to attribute gender to Ricketts' androgynous figures, but in this case there can be no doubt that the one design shows the bare upper torso of a very muscular man, while the other depicts three fully-clad figures moving with a sinuous, but assuredly female, grace.

The most likely explanation is that Ricketts designed from the text, while Granville Barker discovered that, for some purely directorial purpose, possibly the distribution of parts within his company, the play worked better when the

Figure 12.   *Tintagiles*: Servant of the Queen
(Courtesy Bottomley Bequest, Carlisle)

servants were played by male actors. To anyone familiar with Ricketts' rough sketches, it is obvious that his working method was to make quick jottings of ideas which he would then discuss with his director, producer or manager, and then make finished drawings at some later date, especially if there was the opportunity of displaying these designs at an exhibition.[11] Ricketts displayed designs at the International Theatre Exhibition in 1922 and frequently at the Royal Academy annual exhibitions. For such exhibitions he would work and perfect his designs to a point where they became impressive and desirable watercolors in their own right, quite apart from their original, functional purpose, or their value as records of particular productions. This would seem to be the case in this instance. Though the problem is exaggerated by the fact that the Carlisle design is smaller in format than the general run of Ricketts' designs, it appears to date from an earlier period of draftsmanship, while the design for the three female servants is of a later date, having many of the same aesthetic characteristics as the magnificent series of designs Ricketts created in 1924 for Cecil Lewis' unrealized play *Montezuma.*

The design for the three servants of the queen (fig. 13) shows three figures wearing identical costumes which would have been homogenous with those of Ygraine and Bellangère. Over a full black underskirt with long train there is a grey tabard with white stenciled design. Like Ygraine's dress this is fastened at each side by a series of straps at about knee-level. There also seems to be a fastening under the armpit. The cut of this overtunic is rather complicated. Back and front are cut in one piece, rather wide for the shoulders and probably with a simple slit neck. At the front it hangs perfectly straight to a curved hem within six inches of the foot; at the back, the fastenings ensure that the tunic falls as if straight-cut, but, in fact, a great deal more material has been incorporated so that the back hangs in a kind of deep cowl at mid-calf and then tapers off into the train. Obviously this cut would drape magnificently and give a very strange movement to the three characters progressing, as one, across the stage. However, it is a very difficult cut to achieve using a patterned material. Of course, in this case the discussion is hypothetical since the costumes were never realized, but it is a kind of scooped back and train which Ricketts later used frequently, for example, in the *Saint Joan* designs. To the best of my knowledge, however, Ricketts always used this cut with materials he had stenciled himself so that he could "cheat" a little, or with plain fabrics—never with machine woven or printed patterns. Lillah McCarthy unwittingly throws light on the subject when she writes:

> He designed my dresses for many years and he painted most of them. Sometimes he would work so late at night for me that the dress would arrive at the theatre still smelling of its new paint.[12]

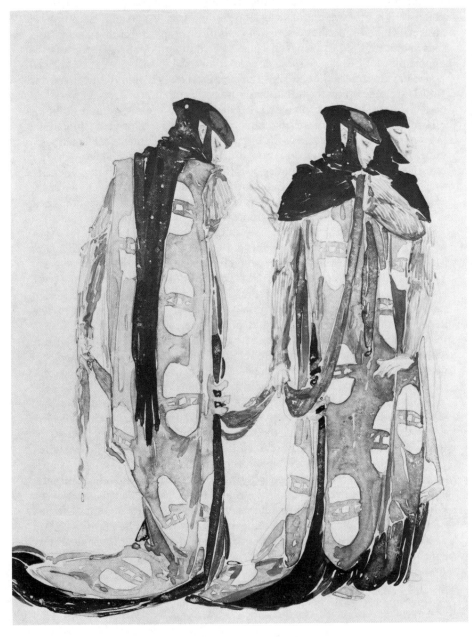

Figure 13.   *Tintagiles*: Servants of the Queen
               (Courtesy Victoria and Albert Museum)

In other words he painted or stenciled at least part of the costumes after they had been made up, which would enable him to get the fullness of cut he desired, while retaining the semblance of regularity in the pattern.

The sleeves of the costumes are tightly cut from a gold and white striped material. The long blood-red sash or rope, which the three figures hold between them, and their headdresses, are the same as those actually used in the production, and depicted in the design for the male version of the costume. It is interesting that this awe-inspiring red rope is not mentioned in the text. Yet it is certainly about to be used for the abduction of the child. Both versions of the design have the same headdress, a flat black hat of a soft, possibly woolen material, worn well forward over the brow, attached to a loose type of Balaclava helmet. The ears, mouth, nose and eyes are exposed, but the chin and neck are covered by a mass of material wound round the neck and shoulders and allowed to hang naturally down the back. In the female costume it gives the sense of a black, medieval wimple for some bizarre order of nuns; in the male costume there is something reminiscent of an executioner's headgear.

The costume for the male figure consists of a narrow strip of dark grey material which passes over the shoulders and under the headdress, and hangs down to about ankle-length in back and in front. The edges are torn in irregular slashes, giving something of the impression of a well-worn blacksmith's apron. The legs, feet and abdomen are covered in black tights, and the lower chest is tightly bound with dark straps which wrap around the body six or seven times, thus holding the back and front of the narrow grey strip together and, at the same time, concealing the top of the tights. The impression is extremely sinister, a feeling that is increased by the wearing of one black, fingerless gauntlet. In the other hand the intriguing dark red strip of fabric is wound menacingly around the bare arm and knuckles. The production photograph (fig. 14) shows a very faithful version of this costume, with the three actors huddled closely together, one of them sporting a large and incongruously modern pair of scissors thrust in his belt.

What is lost by using the male version of the design is an element of pattern, the *frisson* of the creeping almost sensuous sound of the robes sweeping the floor, a cloying, feline sense of death about to spring. What is gained is a feeling of brute strength, of raw aggression. Undoubtedly the female design is closer to the mood of the text, but it is typical of Ricketts and of the type of theatre work in which he was engaged that, in the circumstances of this production, he came up with a compromise which had its own peculiar viability.

This play, which seems unsympathetic, even morbid to a modern reader, obviously manifested a considerable attraction for men and women of the theatre in the early years of this century. Meyerhold and Sapounov, Lugné-Poe and Georgette Leblanc, Granville Barker, Ricketts and Lillah McCarthy all did memorable work in the service of this strange little play.[13] Vaughan Williams

Figure 14.   *Tintagiles*: Servants of the Queen
             (Courtesy Enthoven Collection, Victoria and Albert Museum)

even composed incidental music for the Ricketts production.[14] This strange fascination can be seen as a typical product of the various movements coming together under the general banner of art nouveau. As had been pointed out by many art historians, British manifestations of this style tend away from the willowy excesses of the Continental art nouveau towards a stronger line, a formal elegance—based, perhaps, on the Art and Crafts Movement's celebration of the Viking and Celtic antiquities of Britain.[15] One thinks of the austere spacial control of Charles Rennie Mackintosh's designs, and of his wife's softer, more delicate, decorative panels.[16] I find the same happy combination of elements in this set of Ricketts' designs for *The Death of Tintagiles.* While I do not suggest direct influence in either direction, I find the same concentration of decorative detail in functional elements in the way Ricketts uses layers of belts and fastenings that is evident in the care the Mackintoshes took, for example, over the design of hinges and latches for a cabinet.

Whatever the origins of the stark but haunting beauty of these Ricketts designs, when completed they made an impression which lasted long after their brief hour upon the stage:

> One of the loveliest presentations of a Maeterlinck play is to the credit of Granville Barker— *The Death of Tintagiles.* Lillah McCarthy's playing of Ygraine, sister of the boy, Tintagiles, the music of Vaughan Williams, and the lovely background of scenery and costume by Charles Ricketts were added to the mist-ridden poetry of Maeterlinck. The dramatist wanted his characters to be regarded as puppets rather than as flesh and blood characters, and even suggested that a gauze veil should be spread between the stage and the audience, thus emphasising the aloofness of the characters from the realism of the day-to-day world. Beauty in generous measure was always there, beginning with the stately loveliness of Lillah McCarthy, wearing the wonder-gown, with its medieval, chequer pattern, which Ricketts devised for Ygraine.[17]

Twenty years after the production, Gordon Bottomley still remembered its "subtle and suggestive mounting" and "its memorable, haunting, atmospheric beauty."[18]

4

The Irish Plays (1908-1915)

It is sometimes assumed that the renaissance in Irish drama in the early years of this century took place in Dublin. But, just as a grudging acceptance of the Irish players at home resulted to a large extent from the *succès d'estime* abroad during the United Kingdom and North American tours, so the roots of the resurgence are to be found, not only in the tides of nationalism and pan-Celticism sweeping Ireland, but also in the literary and artistic circles of Paris and London in the 1890s.[1] Ricketts was a central figure among artists and writers in London at this period. Moreover, having spent a considerable part of his early years in France, he maintained contact through travel, social intercourse, correspondence and reading with Continental trends and ideas. During most of Yeats' school days in London, Ricketts would have been abroad, but Yeats visited the studios of artists with his father, the painter John Butler Yeats, so that, though Yeats and Ricketts did not meet until they were both in their midtwenties, they had many of the same haunts and acquaintances among the older generation of artists, such as William Morris and his circle, and among the younger generation of writers, such as Lionel Johnson and the members of the Rhymers Club.[2] Even after Yeats returned to Ireland to live, he remained a frequent visitor to London, and it was inevitable that he would eventually find his way to the Friday evening gatherings at the studio of Ricketts and Shannon:

> Another fanaticism delayed my friendship with two men, who are now my friends and in certain matters my chief instructors. Somebody, probably Lionel Johnson, brought me to the studio of Charles Ricketts and Charles Shannon, certainly heirs of the great tradition....[3]

Yeats is here referring to some period between 1887 and 1891, when both he and Ricketts would have been in their midtwenties, and Shannon a few years older. Yeats quickly established himself as one of the small circle of friends who were encouraged to drop into the studio at any time, rather than being restricted to the weekly "at homes." The young Irishman later introduced Lady Gregory, John Millington Synge and at least one of the Fay brothers to

Ricketts. It was only a matter of time before Ricketts was invited to design some of the productions of the new Irish National Theatre Society.

Ricketts' earliest design project for the new theatre group is referred to in a letter from Yeats dated 26 July 1904, when the poet was staying at Coole Park, Lady Gregory's estate, along with Synge and George Russell, the poet AE:

> My Dear Ricketts,
>   I have been a long time in writing to thank you for having sent me such admirable designs for the Black Jester. I showed them to Frank Fay in Dublin and he was delighted with them. And as soon as I can make some little progress with the poems I have in mind for recitation, I will have the costume made. The Black Jester is one of the characters in a play I am now writing, and for that too the design will serve.[4]

These designs now seem to be lost, which is unfortunate for several reasons, not least of which is the fact that they would appear to have been among Ricketts' earliest attempts at theatrical design.

The early days of the indigent Irish players found Yeats in the slightly embarrassing position of knowing too many artists and potential designers. Apart from those immediately associated with, or related to, the founders— Jack Yeats, Robert Gregory, George Russell (AE) and Miss Horniman—Yeats was also familiar with Ricketts, T. Sturge Moore, Pamela Colman Smith, Elinor Monsell, Althea Gyles and William Rothenstein.[5] Later, through Ricketts, he met Edmund Dulac who designed a drop curtain, costumes and masks for The Hawk's Well. By 1902 Yeats had also met Edward Gordon Craig.

From this welter of young artists it would be difficult to identify specific areas of influence on Yeats' concept of stage design. Even in cases where Yeats has made note of his reactions to a certain designer's work, it is not always clear how much that designer fundamentally shaped Yeats' ideas. It would also be wrong to ignore the influence of other writers, rather than designers, who might have introduced Yeats to new concepts of stage decoration. Not least of this group is Ezra Pound whose interest in oriental literature may have led Yeats to his study of the Japanese Noh drama, with its singular decorative conventions. The much-quoted comment by Yeats, "After us the Savage God," with reference to the first production of Jarry's Ubu Roi and its attendant riots in 1896, reminds one that another formative influence of Yeats' notions of stage design might be found in the many theatrical events he attended in Paris and London, at both established and avant-garde theatres.[6]

In 1900 the Purcell Society gave a production in London of the opera Dido and Aeneas which first brought the designs of Edward Gordon Craig to public attention. Yeats saw a revival of this production in 1901, together with The Masque of Love, and considered that Craig had "created an ideal country where everything is possible, even speaking in verse, or speaking to music, or the expression of the whole life in a dance."[7] Yeats determined to meet Craig.

Accustomed as we now are to the stern image of the mature senator-poet, it is hard to imagine the boyish pluck with which Yeats set out, through his friend Pixie Smith and her friend Edy Craig, the artist's sister, to discover Craig's "little stage dodges" to pass these on to his own company.[8] It was, perhaps, such juvenile plundering of his ideas that turned Craig into the suspicious old man he became, but at first he was enthusiastic and responsive to Yeats, providing him with a model stage with which to lecture his Dublin audiences during the interval between plays on a double-bill.[9] Though Yeats was impressed by Craig's designs, it is doubtful that the designer would have recognized his ideas in the earliest productions of the Irish players which Yeats directed. Such photographs as exist, and Yeats' own guarded disappointment, suggest that the visual aspect was all too amateurish.[10]

The execution of ideas may have been lamentably weak, but Yeats' ideal of stage decoration was fixed, even rigid. By 1903 he could write to his friend T. Sturge Moore, with reference to a set of designs Moore had created for *The Shadowy Waters:*

> My dear Moore,
>   I don't like the colour scheme at all. I know the effect of gauze very well and it will not pull this scheme together.... Your scheme would upset all my criticism here in Dublin. I have been explaining on these principles:
>   1. A background which does not insist on itself and which is so homogenous in colour that it   is always a good background to an actor wherever he stand. Your background is the   contrary to all this.
>   2. Two predominant colours in remote fanciful plays. One colour predominant in actors, one   in backcloth.[11]

It is interesting to note that Yeats is as much concerned with critical consistency as anything else: the design must seem to derive from the theories propounded to his audience—surely enough to try the patience and friendship of any designer other than the gentle Moore. Both of the principles expressed in the letter were common enough in portrait painting and Yeats might have learned them as easily from his father, or during his own irregular attendance at art school, as from Craig.

At this period, during the formative years of the new Irish company, Craig's ideas were not so much a direct influence upon, but rather a catalyst to Yeats, coming between his former experiences of stage design and his struggles with the very limited technical assets of the new group of players. The one idea that struck Yeats most about Craig's work was the bold use of color and lighting to create decorative rather than representational backgrounds. Yet Craig's *Dido and Aeneas,* which had delighted Yeats so much, used a representational background, albeit one broad and suggestive rather than specific and localized in style.[12] There were many reasons for Yeats' avoiding representational back cloths, not the least of which was the tiny stage used at the Molesworth Hall, Dublin, where the earliest productions took place. The stage was no more than sixteen feet wide and eleven feet deep.[13] Under such conditions a representational background could only appear second-rate, at best. When the players moved to the new Abbey Theatre in 1904 the stage was still relatively small: a proscenium opening of twenty-one feet in front of a space forty feet wide from wall to wall with fifteen feet from curtain line to back wall.[14] Dublin had neither the scene-painters nor the technicians required for elaborate stage effects. Nor did the city, so long used to stock touring companies, house commercial suppliers of advanced lighting equipment.[15] Given these limitations, together with the new theatre group's restricted budgets, it was imperative that any theory of staging which tended towards simplicity should be considered. At this opportune juncture Yeats saw Craig's *Dido and Aeneas* revival, and entered into a series of discussions with Craig about stage design.

Whether or not Yeats actually followed Craig's ideas in his early productions is less important than the fact that Craig fired Yeats' imagination. It was not until 1910 when Yeats started to experiment on paper with the idea of screens, and not until 1911 when the actual screens were first used at the Abbey Theatre in a production of Yeats' *The Hour-Glass,* that an identifiably Craigean element can be found in the staging of the Irish plays.[16] There was considerable opposition to the screens among the company, and Joseph Holloway, the inveterate commentator on every aspect of the Abbey's history, was distinctly unimpressed:

> With a great flourish of egotistical trumpets on the part of the management...the Gordon Craig freak scenery and lighting were tried at the Abbey...and while most voted the innovation an affected failure with possibilities for effective stage pictures, none considered it in any way an improvement on the old methods.[17]

The reviewer in *The Irish Times* records a more balanced view, admiring Craig's

> reduction of the stage furniture to its simplest element, so that the figures of the players stand out more prominently against the primitive background and attention is concentrated on the human and truly expressive elements of the drama.[18]

This emphasis on the human and expressive elements is similar to a view expressed by Yeats in a criticism of Craig's lighting as early as 1904:

> He is not greatly interested in the actor, and his streams of coloured direct light, beautiful as they are, will always seem, apart from certain exceptional moments, a new externality. We should rather desire, for all but exceptional moments, an even, shadowless light, like that of noon.[19]

In other words, anything which distracts from the actors, and more especially from the spoken word, is to be avoided.

The screens, together with a very modified version of Craig's lighting ideas, consistent with Yeats' views expressed above and with the limited facilities at the Abbey, served, Yeats hoped, as adjuncts to some ideal imaginative response between audience and stage, a response which focused the audience's attention upon the actors. This kind of directorial criterion throws great emphasis upon the costume design as one of the few remaining possibilities for visual indulgence, together with ritual and ceremony which are in any case, closely related to costume. Yet Roland Barthes reminds us that one must avoid overelaboration of costumes as a kind of visual compensation:

> The costume must always keep its value as a pure function, it must neither smother nor swell the play; it must avoid substituting independent values for the significance of the stage action.[20]

The costumes Ricketts designed for the Irish players achieved this careful balance: exciting enough to concentrate the audience's interest upon the actors while remaining sympathetic to the nature of the plays.

With Craig's screens and Ricketts' costumes Yeats had hit upon a happy combination entirely consistent with his values:

> Only two artists have done good work upon the English stage during my time, Mr. Craig and Mr. Ricketts ... and all that these artists have done has been beauty, some of it magnificent beauty.[21]

In bringing together the designs of the two stage artists whom he most admired, Yeats created a union which Craig and Ricketts did not achieve in reality. Though they knew one another, and Ricketts had at one time made encouraging overtures to the younger artist, Craig's suspiciousness and Ricketts' pride prevented any closer working partnership than that manufactured, after the event, by Yeats when he simply put Craig's screens and Ricketts' costumes together.[22]

Designs for parts of four sets of Ricketts' Irish costumes remain, for the most part in the collection of Miss Anne Yeats: Synge's *The Well of the Saints* (1908 production) and his *Deirdre of the Sorrows* (1910 production), Yeats' *The King's Threshold* (1914 production) and his *On Baile's Strand* (1915 production).

For the first of these plays there are three designs. Figure 15, Molly Byrne, shows a fine figure of a country girl. Ricketts' notes on the drawing read "skirt—limp, no fat petticoat effect" and "apron." The skirt is of a fine, light material such as muslin, gathered simply at the waist. It forms a full skirt, but, because of the limp nature of the fabric, its easy folds cling to the body, emphasizing that sensuous quality in Molly which Timmy and Martin find so irresistable. Molly is well aware of her charms as we learn when she describes herself as "a fine woman, the like of me."[23] As if to stress this flaunting nature in the character, Ricketts paints her holding an apple with one bite missing, for which iconographic prop there is no textual authority. The white skirt is lightly decorated in bands of blue and green flowers. The apron is a long narrow grey strip edged with a dark green pattern and hangs down under the short-sleeved blue jacket which falls loosely around the hips. The jacket is fastened over the breasts with a bow of a paler blue, and bows of this blue are repeated as decoration, one on each side of the neckline. Like the skirt, the jacket appears to be soft and clinging, but not tight, both flattering to the statuesque girl and free enough to accommodate those wilder aspects of Molly's nature which her bare feet betray.

Another design, Molly Byrne in her Wedding Shawl, shows a somewhat tidier Molly. The wedding shawl is related to Timmy's line, "The saint's come to marry the two of us . . . " (III, 137). The second half-view shows the same blue sleeveless jacket with a "green scarf pinned simply" as Ricketts' note states. The full-length view shows Molly wearing the same skirt as before, plus a gold necklace, the blue jacket, green scarf, white stockings, black slippers and the shawl falling demurely from the crown of the head, where it is held in place by a circlet of green leaves. The shawl is a simple semicircle with the straight edge forming the opening. It appears to be lightly stenciled or embroidered in a gold and green curvilinear pattern which has the delicate hint of some ancient Celtic brooch designs. The total effect is one of fine, womanly grace.

The only other design still in existence for this production is titled Timmy the Smith. This is the first design to show Ricketts' rather oriental trousers, which he used for the male characters in all the Irish plays. The pants are cut very wide both at the waist and ankles so that they always have a bunched effect, rather like the fashionable drawstring pants of today. Timmy's trousers are held together at the waist by a rough brown sash and at the ankles by little straps of the same "dirty grey woven fabric of canvas" as the pants, so that they have something of the effect of pants held by cycling clips. Such trousers can easily be adapted to different purposes with the use of various combinations of belts, sashes and leggings. There is nothing particularly archaic or Irish about this design. Yeats' retort to Miss Horniman concerning her design for *On Baile's Strand:*

"Hang archeology!" said the great W.B. Yeats. "It's effect we want on the stage!"

as reported by Holloway, reveals that the poet-director was not concerned with historical accuracy.[24] By careful variation of this basic trouser pattern Ricketts always achieved some sense of distant period and far-off place in the heroic limbo of Yeats' imagination, particularly appropriate for

Figure 15.   Irish Plays: Molly Byrne
(Courtesy Anne Yeats)

the poet cannot evoke a picture to the mind's eye if a second-rate painter has set his imagination of it before the bodily eye; but decoration and suggestion will accompany our moods, and turn our minds to meditation, and yet never become obtrusive or wearisome.[25]

Timmy also wears a black shirt which Ricketts' note described as "rough woolen stuff." The sleeves are rolled back revealing the brawny arms demanded by the lines:

> Its well you know Timmy the smith has a great strength in his arm, and its a power of things it has broken.... [III, 123]

The strong neck bursts through the lacing at the chest. The whole costume is topped with a rather strange fezlike cap of an orange and white material. It seems almost too small for the great bulk of the head, and suggests that Ricketts wanted Timmy to look slightly ridiculous. Ricketts notes against the cap "stuff to be supplied" and "£.10, Morgan," the latter of which defies explanation.[26]

Ricketts never visited Ireland, so far as is known. When any of his designs had to be executed in Dublin rather than in London, he seems to have sent rather optimistic instructions as to technique. In the case of this play a letter from Yeats to Synge survives in which Ricketts' instructions are relayed:

> He wants the execution of the designs to be as vague as possible. Shawn, he says, should first paint it all in and then sponge over the details. It should all be scenery low in tone—lower in tone than anything he ever did. When he wants to darken he should glaze with size or scramble it over. He is not giving minute measurements. Shawn must follow the designs so as to get the general effect as broadly and simply as possible. He is to use blue and violet in the shadows as well as brown and make the base of all the stones and the trunks green as if they were grown where they touch the ground. The glen should be improvised by a green floor cloth—at the borders seeming grey. Plants at the bottom of the backcloth can be changed to evening by a change of light. Green and black and dark blue should be the clothes of the persons. Bush and piece of ruined wall should be one piece but can be made up to whatever height fits the height of your two players.[27]

From these second-hand instructions plus the three costume designs it is difficult to judge the complete effect Ricketts hoped to achieve, yet one may be forgiven for inferring a general impression of vigorous line and delicate color. And perhaps it is not altogether too far-fetched to construe signs of that same joy in "imagination that is fiery and magnificent, and tender" which Synge had expressed the previous year in his preface to *The Playboy of the Western World*.[28]

Ricketts designed costumes for Synge's *Deirdre of the Sorrows* for the first Abbey production in 1910, a year after Synge's death. The production was codirected by Maire O'Neill (Molly Allgood) who also played Deirdre. Robert Gregory designed the sets. Three of Ricketts' costume designs are known to have survived.

Deirdre and Lavarcham, a rough pen and watercolor sketch torn from a roll of rather flimsy paper, shows the corner of another costume at one edge. This would indicate that for these rough drawings Ricketts worked in a strip which he later chopped up into individual drawings. Lavarcham wears a rough, reddish-brown skirt and blouse and a white apron printed with a blue geometric pattern. Ricketts notes "apron of printed cotton *washed*," stressing that the apron should appear old and worn. A green drawstring bag is suspended from the waist on a long cord or string. Lavarcham wears two shawls, a black and a white, the white one having a hood. Ricketts notes "white shawl worn over black shawl," and "white shawl and apron not worn after Act I." The white shawl looks like a soft woolen fabric, cut in a full circle with a gathered hood bagged out over the shoulders. The shawl is fastened at the neck by two gold discs, which a later design informs us are made from twists of gold rope. This decorative fastening, reminiscent of the impact of Viking arts on medieval Irish artifacts, is one of the few indications of specific period in the costume.[29] It is, in fact, as well that Lavarcham starts out the play wearing both shawls, as this helps to establish period. Once she removes the top shawl and the white apron she will present a study in black and brown. There is surely an intended contrast in this because Lavarcham moves from a bright, cozy look to a dark appearance while Deirdre progresses from a worn and careless attire to rich and queenly dress. The effect of Deirdre's transformation would be rendered all the more striking by contrast with her companion. Lavarcham walks with a stick or possibly a crutch. The weight of the figure is certainly carried on this prop. Perhaps Ricketts, knowing that most of the Abbey actresses were very young girls, added this hint of the character's age to help the actress create the right impression.[30]

Deirdre's costume in the same sketch shows a barefoot girl in ragged clothing trailing a massive sword in one hand. Her wild hair is tied back with a band of striped material. She wears a loose-fitting brown jacket with short sleeves, similar to the blue jacket worn by Molly, discussed above. Despite its rough, country look it is of a flattering enough cut to justify Naisi's fatal attraction to Deirdre, after catching a mere glimpse of her in the forest. The skirt or underdress is of a light material, possibly muslin, in white covered with irregular flecks of red. On one knee there is a patch of blue, or possibly a hole revealing a blue underskirt. A narrow apron similar to Molly Byrne's, except white with an olive green border, hangs in front of the dress. The figure is drawn showing an awkward bravado consistent with the character; she knows her own mind and will stand her ground, yet she has the shyness of a young girl reared in seclusion far from the sight of men. Though this is only a rough sketch, it shows a careful reading of the text, suggesting the strength, defiance and independence of the two women, but with an indication of their deep affection in the way they lean towards one another protectively.

Figure 16, Deirdre Acts II and III, reveals Ricketts at his most inventive. The immediate problem with this costume is a financial one. The actual transformation in Deirdre's appearance takes place towards the end of Act I: *"Deirdre comes in on left royally dressed and very beautiful"* (IV, 207). Obviously she is now wearing "the rich dresses and jewels have been sent from Emain" (IV, 199). The design budgets of the Irish Players were minuscule.[31] Ricketts therefore had to create the illusion of a rich, bejeweled costume without involving much actual expense. A further requirement, which a hasty designer might miss, is that the dress must eschew any gaudy vulgarity. The first words she speaks in the new costume are "Naisi.... Do not leave me, Naisi, I am Deirdre of the Sorrows" (IV, 207). An editorial gloss in the *Collected Works* reads:

> Synge has scribbled beside Deirdre's entrance in TS'H' (15 February 1908) the following description, "her excitement turned into a sort of dignity which is new and surprising to herself." [IV, 206]

In other words, while the costume must seem rich it also must be dignified, adding something to the weight of anticipation in that fate-defying, essential sobriquet, "I am Deirdre of the Sorrows." Ricketts has chosen the somber richness of pale blue, bottle green, dark brown and grey. The long blue skirt falls over and around the feet in languid folds. The material may be velvet as the sketch shows the deep, cast shadows which are characteristic of that fabric. Over this comes a white, sleeveless tunic, which in turn covers a dark green undergarment, of which only one long fitted sleeve and a little triangular section at the neck can be seen. The white tunic is decorated by a braid at the neck opening, and by a deep border, both of the same dark green as the undergarment. The patterned border is presumably printed, stenciled or appliqued. Without any attempt at deceit, this decorative border gives the sense of jewelry studding the hem of the tunic. Actual jewelry is confined to a number of heavy dark-colored rings. The master stroke of the design is the long stole which is thrown over the back of the head and falls to the floor on either side of the figure. Its ample folds would easily conceal the knife required at the end of the play. Ricketts' notes on the drawing read "grey Ribledale [sic] sheeting" and "this will be here tomorrow." The material is narrowly striped in pale grey and dark brown. Richness is conveyed by the sheer extent of it and also by the optical effect that such striped fabrics have on stage, where they appear to ripple and scintillate like heavy silken plush.[32] Assuming that the lighting effects, suggesting the distant burning of Emain which end the play, could be achieved, the impression of Deirdre's final lines, her suicide and gradual sinking into the grave of Naisi and his brothers, would have a near Wagnerian magnificence with Deirdre's stole flashing a dull, watery reflection of the distant flames. From cheap materials Ricketts' design suggests the necessary sense of queenly luxury while retaining the dignity Synge's note requires. The figure's Madonnalike posture and the stole's heavy, drooping lines and somber colors epitomize Deirdre's fate and foreshadow the well-known consequences of her tragedy, so that in the closing moments of the play the great, dimly glowing stole would seem to enfold all the sorrows of Ireland.[33]

The Conchobor design is merely a sketch of a red cloak with gold and black decoration. There is also a helmet of the same red, and a working drawing for this headgear. The cloak is typical of many Ricketts designed for the Abbey players. Conscious, as always, of economic considerations, he notes on this sketch "house flannel," in other words, the basic material to be used for this and most of the Irish costumes is the ordinary cheap flannel which has been used for petticoats and nightshirts since at least as long ago as the seventeenth century, the same red fabric used for the Aran girls' skirts in Synge's *Riders to the Sea*. Because this flannel has a slight pile when new, many designers with restricted budgets hope that, with proper lighting, it might give the impression of velvet. Perhaps Ricketts shared this optimism when he designed this costume for the High King of Ulster, but it is more likely that he was mindful of its other qualities. Provided it is properly lined, so that it does not stick to itself, and weighted, flannel hangs well, and since it is one of the cheapest materials available, it can be used extravagantly so that great folds of the fabric give a feeling of ample richness. It also washes well, fades naturally in sunlight, and for stage purposes, can be artificially aged easily and convincingly. In Conchobor's costume it is cut in the classic full-circle cape; a pattern ancient, simple and practical. It has a very full, gathered hood which lies loosely about the neck forming a large collar, and is secured at the neck by the twists of gold rope which Ricketts used repeatedly in these Irish costumes. The gold is repeated in the great decorative panel of black, white and gold. This is made up of two semicircles, one on each side of the front opening, so that when the two sides are joined it forms a complete circle, having a certain resemblance to a ceremonial shield. The decoration is not particularly Celtic in conception. Like most other panels of this kind in the Irish designs, it is rectilinear, abstract, avoiding close identification with any particular source. A note on another of these designs reads "Furniture satin," which helps to explain the geometric nature of these designs; they are not stenciled as one might expect from familiarity which Ricketts' methods, but appliqued from small pieces of rich material. These would be much easier to work in square or oblong patches. The contrast of smooth black and gold satin on a white background, against the soft red flannel, must have gone a long way to making this humble fabric look suitably proud and regal for Conchobor. The helmet of the same red color has a pointed crown which looks appropriately ancient. It is decorated with the same twists of gold rope as the familiar neck fastening. The pencil sketch of the helmet suggests one or two golden feathers. There is no indication of what is worn under the cloak but it was undoubtedly trousers of the same pattern as Timmy the Smith's in *The Well of the Saints*. Surprisingly enough Conchobor is shown as a relatively young man with jet black beard and moustache. One

Figure 16.   Irish Plays: Deirdre, Acts II and III
(Courtesy Anne Yeats)

can only imagine that Ricketts had not read the description *"Conchobor, High King of Ulster, about sixty"* in the limited Cuala edition of the same year (1910). Indeed, he may have been working from a typed script without a cast list. It is also conceivable that, given the youthfulness of the Abbey company, Ricketts thought a full black beard enough to separate the brimming pubescence of Naisi and Deirdre from the poignant maturity of Conchobor.

Ricketts designed costumes for Yeats' *The King's Threshold* for the Abbey company's visit to the Royal Court Theatre, London, in June 1914. By this time the Abbey was in possession of the variable screens designed by Craig. In Ireland, this play would have been performed in the scenery devised from Craig's screens, but Craig withheld permission for the screens to be used outside of Ireland. Therefore in the United Kingdom and in North America the company had to make do with such scenery as they could find, most often a simple arrangement of traverse curtains together with a few stock pieces such as steps and door frames. No evidence remains of what scenery was used on this occasion. A design for a painted back cloth, dated 1913, by Jack Yeats for *The King's Threshold* exists in the National Gallery of Ireland, but there is nothing to suggest that it was used for the London production.[34] It is unfortunate that Craig's injunction deprived so many audiences outside Ireland of the chance to see the full glory of Ricketts' costumes in the settings derived from Craig's invention, which Yeats conceived as their proper framework.

Five Ricketts designs for costumes in this play are known to exist.

Figure 17, King Guaire, shows a mature, rather cowed figure—the king at the end of the play, humbled by the unbending will of the poet Seanchan. The undergarment is an ankle-length green tunic. There are irregular patches of pattern at the knee, under the arm and around the upper sleeve. The figure is stout as if Ricketts is pointing out some constrast to the build of the emaciated poet who is dying of self-starvation. The king's waist is made even bulkier by a patch of brown fur which Ricketts indicates as "animal baize" bound to the waist by a white sash. Over the tunic is a white cloak cut in a full circle. As with the Conchobor design of four years earlier, Ricketts notes the material as "house flannel." This would be the kind of cheap white flannel used for baby clothing. The cloak is overlaid with a gold and black appliqued design in squares. This checkered effect is concentrated in a deep band at the neck, two oblong sections at the hem on either side of the front opening and in a long strip falling over the arm, which may, in fact, continue over most of the back. The costume has an opulent, almost Byzantine look, perhaps as a result of the mosaiclike sections of decoration. There are two smaller patches of black and gold pattern in the middle of the remaining white sections of the cloak. Ricketts notes that the patterned sections are "Furniture satin." The king wears a high crescent of gold rope bound layer above layer to form a tiara or crown, and at least one heavy, circular earring of the same material. His full russet beard and hair are divided into sections, some of which are bound with white braids. A

Figure 17.   Irish Plays: King Guaire
(Courtesy Ann Yeats)

further touch of luxury is given by the white boots with center seams of the same green as the tunic. In his hand he carries a long tapered staff, carmine with bands of gold. One imagines the gross weight of the man dragging around with the aid of this colorful, almost ironic, prop of kingly office. The beseeching glance of the eyes is emphasized by the dark arched brows and the pink flush of the high cheekbones.

As we have noticed before Ricketts often used his costume designs as studies towards characterization. He and Yeats had frequent discussions about the plays and this characterizing aspect in the designs is obviously the result of their close rapport. Writing to thank Ricketts, Yeats concludes:

> I think the costumes the best stage costumes I have ever seen. They are full of dramatic invention, and yet nothing starts out, or seems eccentric. The company never did the play so well, and such is the effect of costume that whole scenes got a new intensity, and passages or actions that had seemed commonplace became powerful and moving.[35]

Quite apart from the encouragement of such an appreciation, Ricketts worked for Yeats in the knowledge that, at least in some form, his designs would reach the stage. Cancellation of projected designs was such a common feature of Ricketts' stage work that it is hardly surprising to find him putting so much of himself into the Irish designs. About the same time as he was working on *The King's Threshold* designs, he notes in his journal that twenty-two costumes he had designed for a new play of J.M. Barrie's have been unnecessary, as the production has been canceled:

> Curiously enough I did not feel particularly angry. In working for the theatre I realised the technical difficulties surrounding every detail owing to people who do not know their business, who won't learn, or who can't afford to give the time it requires to modify their routine.[36]

Despite the resigned tone of these remarks such wasted efforts repeated frequently have a certain numbing effect on a designer's work. On the other hand a complimentary rush of creativity occurs when one knows that creative effort will be fulfilled. Such was the case when Ricketts worked for Yeats and this circumstance goes some way to explaining the extra pains Ricketts took in his designs to indicate character to the actors.

We can apply this characterizing aspect in an attempt to identify the design simply labeled "King's Threshold" in the Victoria and Albert Museum, figure 18. It shows a pompous, strutting fellow with a pouting, condescending look, a curl to his lip. This would suggest the mayor of Kinvara, a part originally created for the comedic arts of Willie Fay.[37] The man's costume is fussy but not kingly, and he carries a thin, uneven stick which could be the prop referred to in the stage direction *"Mayor. (Who carries an Ogham stick)."*[38] In the drawing, the character's hand partly obscures the handle, but it appears to bear the perpendicular notches which could be the ancient Oghamistic Gaelic signs from which the mayor reads his speech in this, Yeats' hardly subtle joke at civic bumbling. The green speckled baggy pants gathered into little flounces at the ankles, and the tiny red slippers have a silly, clownish look lacking in other designs which use the same basic trouser pattern. The man also wears a short, sleeveless, white tunic held tightly to the waist by a broad sash in such a way that the part below the sash skirts out over the hips and thighs. The bold lozenge-shaped gold design increases the bulky, overstuffed look. Assuming that the materials used are the same as in the rest of this series of designs, the sash will be brown baize, and this material is repeated in the trimming of the hem. Over it all he wears a light cape of a striped green and white material. The cloak is different in length and design from that of the various kings in the other Irish costumes, coming to just below the knee, cut square, simply gathered and folded at the neck, then thrown back over the shoulders. It is fastened by a tiny ring, the familiar twisted rope jewelry being merely decorative in this instance. He also wears a dark-colored ring, a pewter bracelet and a circlet of gold rope decorated with red stones upon his head.

Another possibility is that this design represents the king's chamberlain. The drawing of four kings, figure 21, discussed below, has a note "Youngest King: Tunic of Chamberlain *(King's Threshold)*" which refers to this same tunic with its brown sash and lozenge-shaped pattern, as worn by the youngest figure in the group. If the separate design in the Victoria and Albert, figure 18, does show the chamberlain, the wand could be his *"long staff"* mentioned in the stage directions, though it is not, in fact, very long. In any case my remarks about characterization would apply equally well to this royal official and poetaster, representing those government-sponsored versifiers whom Seanchan in the play and Yeats in real life despised:

> Chamberlain.   It is the men who are learned in the laws,
> Or have led the King's armies that should sit
> At the King's table. Nor has poetry
> Been altogether driven away, for I
> As you should know, have written poetry,
> And often when the table has been cleared
> And candles lighted, the King calls for me
> And I repeat it him.   [pp. 39-40][39]

Whether this figure represents the mayor of Kinvara or the King's chamberlain, the design is a convincing medievalization of a certain type of self-important civil servant scorned by both Yeats and Ricketts, and a useful guide to any actor representing the type.

Miss Anne Yeats possesses a delightful design for one of the two young princesses in *The King's Threshold*, inscribed "To Lady Gregory from her admirer Charles Ricketts." The drawing has the delicate grace of some figure

Figure 18.   Irish Plays: [Mayor of Kinvara]
            (Courtesy Victoria and Albert Museum)

from a fairy tale. The main aspect of the costume is a tightly fitting white jacket with a wide skirt, not unlike the cut of some eighteenth-century male ballet dress. It has the same stenciled pattern as Ygraine's dress in *The Death of Tintagiles* (discussed on p. 48 above) except that, in this case the repeat is regular and the pattern is smaller in scale. Under the jacket she wears a long-trained skirt of red and white flecked material which parts at the front to reveal a tiny green slipper. The dropped waist is emphasized with a blue sash, the open neckline with a narrow white collar and a gold pendant. The headdress is a high white turban, like the broad end of an inverted cone rising from the crown of the head. It has some inconspicuous gold decoration. Under the headdress and concealing most of the hair is a massive red veil which falls back from the face and over the shoulders. She wears gloves of a matching red. This graceful costume would be even more appealing when duplicated for the second young princess in the play. The demure elegance of such a pair would make Seanchan's blunt refusal of their youthful pleas all the more shocking, reinforcing the audience's previous impression of his single-minded determination.

The exhibition catalogue *Stage Design at the Abbey Theatre* (Peacock Theatre, Dublin, July 1967) identifies another sketch, the pen-and-ink drawing labeled "King," as being for *The King's Threshold,* but as there is only one king in this play, King Guaire, whose costume has already been discussed, this other drawing must be a working sketch, probably for one of the costumes Ricketts designed the following year for the many kings in *On Baile's Strand.* Also in this catalogue is an entry for the intriguing pen-and-ink sketch *"Angus,"* identifying this as being for *The King's Threshold.* There is no character named Angus in this or any other play by Yeats or Synge. In Yeats' poems the name is always spelt "Aengus," whereas, in the sketch, Ricketts has written "Angus." Ricketts' spelling was always idiosyncratic, so this might be considered a spelling mistake on his part, if only such a Yeatsian character existed.

It is possible that the costume was intended for the reading of some fragment of a play, or a narrative poem such as *Baile and Aillinn,* which could have been read by some actor dressed as Aengus, the mythical Celtic poet.[40] One is also tempted to speculate that this could be the lost design for that other poet-narrator, the black jester. However, Ricketts' notes on this black and white sketch indicate a costume of green and grey; "green cap," "grey cloak thrown over shoulder," "green trousers" and "please return to Mrs. Champion as they [the costumes] are unfinished."[41] A more likely explanation is that Ricketts simply confused the poet Aengus, which he spells "Angus," familiar to him from Yeats' early poems such as *The Song of Wandering Aengus,* with the poet Seanchan in this play. Seanchan's use of bird imagery and the stage directions, *"Seanchan holds up his hand as if a bird perched upon it. He pretends to stroke the bird"* (p. 44), could also have caused Ricketts' mind to slip back to the poet Aengus whom Yeats so often described as being surrounded by a flight of tiny birds. The fact that this rough sketch contains both an ink blot and a run would indicate that it was dashed off very quickly, which might also explain the confusion of "Angus" for Seanchan. Despite these faults of draftsmanship the sketch depicts a suitable costume for the proud, dying poet in *The King's Threshold*. The bulky grey cloak could be worn in such a way as to conceal most of the actor's body and acquiesce in the necessary illusion of starvation. The tightly bound green trousers would make possible the stage direction, *"Seanchan has been dragged some feet, clinging to the Monk's habit"* (p. 43), which would be very clumsy if performed in loose or open-legged pants. A further indication that this might be the design for Seanchan can be found in the design for Cuchulain in *On Baile's Strand*, figure 22, Cuchulain in his Sea Cloak, discussed below. For this production Ricketts reused as many of the earliest costumes as possible. The notes of the Cuchulain design read "underdress that of Seanchan," the underdress in this case being a green tunic and green pants bound at the ankles, more loosely than in the "Angus" sketch, but, as we have already seen, this was a simple matter to achieve.

Some impression of how the other characters in *The King's Threshold* were dressed can be gathered from the notes on the costumes for *On Baile's Strand*. It would seem that the poet's disciples were dressed in high white caps, green tunics and loose white pants bound at the ankles, and they wore white cloaks thrown over their shoulders.

In May and June of 1915 there was a return visit to London by the Abbey company, playing this time at the Little Theatre. Ricketts designed costumes for *On Baile's Strand* building upon the stock he had already created. A letter from Lady Gregory refers to these designs: "I have seen your beautiful new designs. How good you are! They are wonderful."[42] Ricketts attended the London rehearsals. His journal entry for 18 May 1915 gives some indication of the complexity of resentments within the company. Yeats was absent from London and Lady Gregory, still in a state of shock over the drowning of her nephew Hugh Lane in the Lusitania disaster, was having difficulty with the players. Ricketts took command of the situation and it is interesting to note his perception and diplomacy as he rises above his own immediate concerns, the unpopularity of his costumes:

Rehearsal of the *Well of the Saints*. Poor Lady Gregory, looking singularly cowed and aged, was in the stalls. I praised her play and discussed the acting, which had been very bad. The players, not the girls, resented and disliked their dresses and were in a sort of rebellion, Sinclair, the comedian, who is troublesome just now, having led the strike. I praised the women, suggesting the toning down of things. Gradually the hostility wore off. I praised Morgan's acting to him; he then unburdened himself and confessed they were hostile to Lady Gregory's new play, did not like it, or want to act in it. I, of course, praised the play and said they had seemed to me below the average and to have acted with hesitation. In the evening, everyone wore their dresses and the play went admirably.[43]

By 1907 Yeats had changed the text of *On Baile's Strand* so as to introduce three singing women. Earlier productions, based on the 1904 edition of the play, would have been entirely masculine affairs. The 1915 London production of the play included this strange, new, female element.[44] The rest of the costumes consolidated the general line and color scheme of *The King's Threshold*. The only character for whom no costume design has survived is the young man, Cuchulain's son.

The comic framework of the play is carried by the blind man, Fintain, and the fool, Barach. There are individual sketches for each and a composite design showing Fintain groping his way forward while Barach comes behind, apparently teasing his partner, figure 19, Blind Man and Fool. The sketch named Blind Man includes a side view showing the hang of the rather oriental black pants. Over the pants he wears a plain, square-cut black tunic with a ragged hem. On the chest there is a sky-blue patch which gives an extraordinary touch of pathos, especially as the eyes are bound with a rough black handkerchief. Ricketts' notes read "blue patch" and "bandaged hand" and on the head "black sash on eyes," "white space" and "wig or cap." The "white space" refers to the break in black between the binding on the eyes and the start of the black "cap or wig." It is a stylized version of blindness, but a very moving one.

The fool is dressed in a mixture of orange, brown, dirty red and green. The notes read "yellow linen stenciled green," "green baize" referring to the peaked cap, "animal baize" against the rough brown apron in front, and "dirty red" referring to the leggings. He also carries a stick with colored streamers and is covered in belts and bindings, suitable places for concealing all his stolen food.

While these two add comic relief, the three singing women give a sense of mystery or fate, figure 20, Singing Women. They wear long trailing tunics of a deep, bottle green with black yokes and black, geometrically shaped decorations. They are barefoot. The three costumes are identical and the main item of each costume is the headdress, a pointed cap with the same white material flowing in loose folds over the shoulders and down to midcalf, the whole held in place by great knotted sheets of flimsy scarlet material, which not only bind cap to head and chin but are tied so as to flop out over the ears and then to fall freely to their frayed edges. One of the women holds a bowl of fire and another a sprig of herbs to cast upon the flames. These costumes for this momentary appearance would be easy and inexpensive to make, yet they would cast an otherworldly spell upon the scene, consistent with Yeats' intention in introducing this new element to his play. The knotted scarlet of the headdresses is one of the few touches of color in the production, beyond the range of white, green and grey, except for such occasional decorative touches as spears. Glimpsed but briefly, performing their strange rite, the three women with their sudden burst of blood red indicate a symbolic use of color foreshadowing the death of the young man.

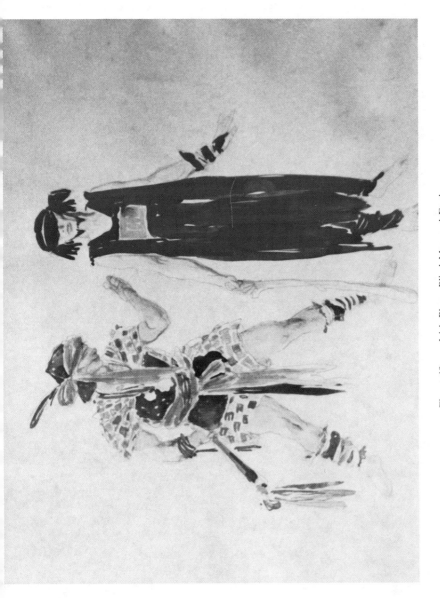

Figure 19.   Irish Plays: Blind Man and Fool
            (Courtesy Anne Yeats)

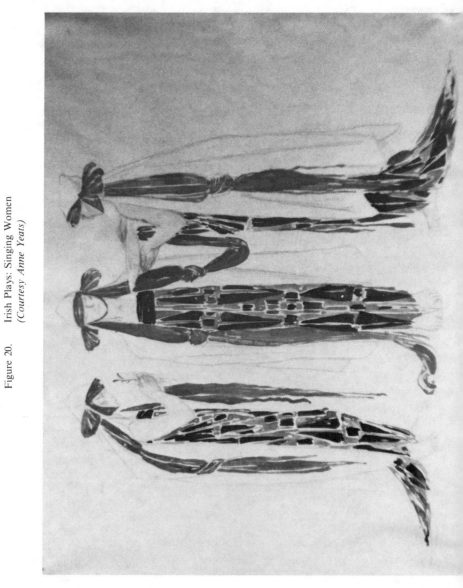

Figure 20.   Irish Plays: Singing Women
(Courtesy Anne Yeats)

The composite design for four kings, figure 21, Four Kings, is a fund of information about the economy with which Ricketts "shuffled" the costumes from the previous year:

> Old King: Disciple's cap (King's Threshold): new cloak (grey): underdress from Green Helmet.
>
> Middle Aged King: Disciple's cap: new cloak, underdress (Green Helmet).
>
> Youngest King: Disciple's cap (King's Threshold): Tunic of Chamberlain (King's Threshold): Disciple's Trousers and cloak worn free.
>
> Young King: Disciple's dress (King's Threshold): new headdress.

This design and three working drawings for cloaks give the general green, grey and white color scheme with decorative details of gold and black. The long spears and the young king's headdress add touches of red which, together with the brief appearance of the three singing women, would provide the only contrast to the general scheme. The only other known design for this production is figure 22, Cuchulain in his Sea-Cloak. Ricketts' notes on the design read: "New cap," "new cloak," "fur gauntlet," "fur band" and "underdress that of Seanchan." The new cap is a black pointed helmet decorated with gold discs, three bands of gold and red feathers. The underdress has been discussed with reference to Seanchan. The "fur gauntlet" is bound to the lower arm with gold rope and emphasizes the exposed, muscular arm and shoulder. The "fur band" is a broad girdle which binds the waist of the green tunic. Around his neck Cuchulain wears a heavy gold necklace. The sea-cloak is a magnificent creation befitting all the poetry that is associated with it:

> *Cuchulain:*   I'll give you gifts
> That Aoife'll know and all her people know
> To have been my gifts. Mananan, son of the seas,
> Gave me this heavy embroidered cloak
> Nine Queens
> Of the Land-under-Waves have woven it
> Out of the fleeces of the sea....   [pp. 99-100]
>
> Cliodna embroidered these bird wings, but Fand
> Made all these little golden eyes with the hairs
> That she had stolen out of Aengus' beard
> And therefore none that has this cloak about him
> Is crossed in love. The heavy inlaid brooch
> That Buan hammered has a merit too.
> *(He begins spreading the cloak out on a bench....)*   [p. 103]

Not only is the cloak examined closely by those on stage, but, left behind on stage, first when Cuchulain and the young man go off to fight, and finally when Cuchulain, mad with grief makes his final exit, it forms a visual attraction for

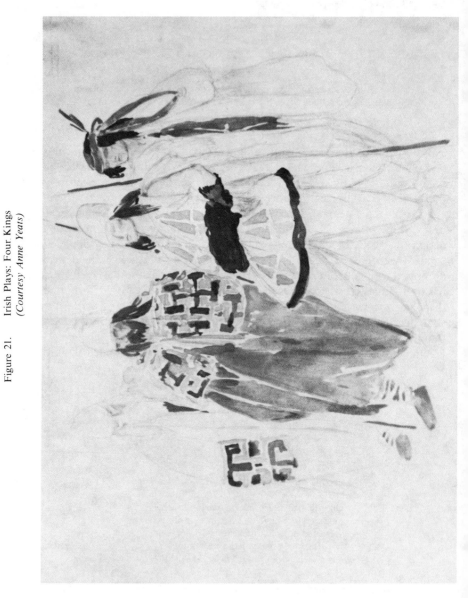

Figure 21. Irish Plays: Four Kings
(Courtesy Anne Yeats)

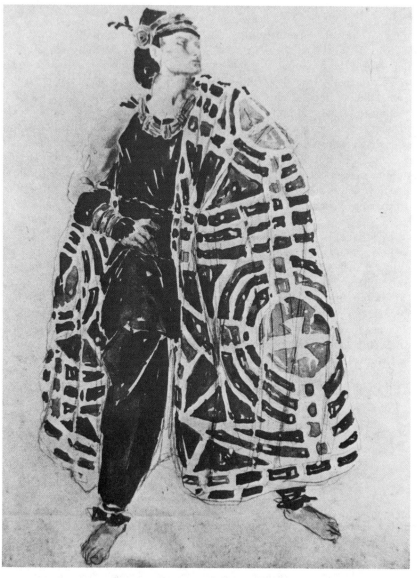

Figure 22.   Irish Plays: Cuchulain in His Sea-Cloak
(Courtesy Anne Yeats)

the audience. In fact, at this point, the sea-cloak comes very close to the ceremonial cloth of the curtain dance from oriental theatre with which both Yeats and Gordon Bottomley experimented, or to the use of masks when, as in O'Neill's *The Great God Brown,* mask and character are emblems of one another. Thus the great sea-cloak, with all its weight of past glory, left abandoned on stage, is emblematic of the wandering, confused, loveless Cuchulain, as he goes out to kill the young man, not knowing him to be his own son, and yet again, when knowing the full horror of what he has done, he strides off into the sea depths. This interpretation can only be speculative, since the directions in the text are very brief, but it is certainly not impossible that Yeats had such an iconographic intention for the elaborate garment spread out upon its bench. Certainly Ricketts' twisting, swirling pattern when spread out would have suggested both the tossing of the sea waves and the turmoil of tragic emotions in the play. There is also great dramatic irony in the fact that the little golden eyes embroidered on the garment as a charm against being "crossed in love" have protected no one—Aoife, Cuchulain or the offspring of their brief joy.

Like the other cloaks in the play the sea-cloak is cut in a full circle. Green and gold appliqued or embroidered decorations almost completely cover it. To embroider such a costume entirely would have been a massive undertaking and it seems likely that a combination of applied patches and embroidery were used, despite the relative difficulty of applying larger curvilinear sections. The white background forms a regular outline to the various decorative pieces, so that it has the total effect of some vast and ancient motif from an illuminated manuscript. One only hopes that, though no specific stage direction to the effect is given, some actor had the chance to display it.

Looking back upon the whole history of costume design at the Abbey Theatre, Lennox Robinson wrote:

> In the matter of scenery—unrealistic scenery...we have compromised to our own satisfaction by the use of a set of screens devised a good many years ago by Mr. Gordon Craig. They are easy to handle and capable of being arranged in an endless number or combinations, in fifteen years we have not exhausted their uses, practically all our "romantic" scenes are created out of them, they are as versatile as our players.
>
> In the matter of costume something equivalent to these screens must be sought by a repertory theatre.... For such [romantic] plays something as malleable and versatile as Mr. Gordon Craig's screens must be looked for, something that can be easily altered and interchanged. The screens are very simple in line and colour; they can hardly be made to look odd and wrong; costume is more elaborate, more varied in colour, and it is very easy to go wrong.
>
> But economy—compromise of some sort—is imperative and the designs of Mr. Ricketts, which illustrate this article, show how beautifully it can be achieved. They were made many years ago for our theatre, for the production of Mr. W.B. Yeats's poetical plays, for "The King's Threshold," "On Baile's Strand" and "The Green Helmet" in particular; in point of fact they have served as a stock of costumes in which any of Mr. Yeats's poetical plays can be

performed. Naturally each of these plays will be likely to demand a dress or two peculiar to itself, the little princesses in "The King's Threshold," the singing women in "On Baile's Strand" are in a sense, "peculiar"—but nearly all the other dresses are composite. Looking at Mr. Ricketts' notes on the costumes for Old, Middle-aged and Youngest King in the latter play, I see that he indicates that their caps are the pupils' caps out of "The King's Threshold".... Even when Mr. Ricketts designs a costume for the hero of "The Green Helmet" he uses the same careful economy, and the dress under Cuchulain's great sea-cloak is that of the dying poet Seanchan.

But the beauty of these dresses and our theatre's poverty have made us use them for purposes that Mr. Ricketts, perhaps, never dreamed of. This large set of costumes, has in fact, furnished us with a wardrobe of beautiful stock "romantic" costumes as adaptable as Mr. Gordon Craig's screens. On their variety and richness it has been possible to draw to an almost unlimited extent. We dressed Lady Gregory's fantastic play "The Dragon" from them and the singing women's dresses which seemed peculiar to "On Baile's Strand" turned out to be perfect costumes for the little prince's fantastic aunts.[45]

The rest of Robinson's article makes a comparison between costumes limited to one play and Ricketts' notion of stock costumes, for example, a king's robe that serves for the king in all plays.

The designs for the Irish plays were not the only set of interchangeable stock costumes created by Ricketts. In 1918 he created costumes and scenery for *Twelfth Night, The Merchant of Venice* and *Two Gentlemen of Verona,* on the same principle for the performances given by Lena Ashwell's company for the British Army stationed in France. In an unpublished letter to Lillah McCarthy, he compares this design project with the Irish costumes:

I am working hand over hand in designing dresses and curtain settings for "Twelfth Night," "Two Gentlemen of Verona" and "The Merchant of Venice" for the Y.M.C.A. Hut performances in France. Out of 30 dresses I make over 50, by transporting cloaks, doublets, etc., and not only does the trick not show, but the persons keep character, and some of the combinations are splendid. I did this for Yeats once for his "King's Threshold" & "Baile's Strand" and, for an emergency single performance, reshuffled the dresses for Synge's "Deirdre of the Sorrows."[46]

His enthusiasm for this reshuffling of stock is given further expression in a letter to Lawrence Binyon:

I am working with both hands on dresses, etc., for *Twelfth Night, Merchant of Venice,* and *Two Gentlemen of Verona.* The third play is made by transposition of other dresses, yet the Illyrians and Elizabethans of *Twelfth Night* are invisible in the other two plays, where I introduce a Giorgione and early Titian element. Sir Andrew Aguecheek has a doublet embroidered with grapes, squirrels and butterflies; the Prince jewelled gloves. Shylock is terrific. Portia has a dress covered with mermaids, Jessica wears the Oriental garb of the Jewesses in Bellini and Carpaccio, I have introduced the striped dress of the *Mass of Bolsena* and Titain's Paduan frescoes, some persons have arabesques on their tights and gold wings on their hats. The plays are for the Y.M.C.A. Hut performances at Le Havre and Paris. Shannon agrees the designs are perhaps my best.[47]

As with the Irish plays Ricketts did some of his finest stage designs when faced with very limited means and the additional problems of interchangeable costumes. His enthusiasm in both instances was directly related to the certainty that the designs would be used and that his efforts would be appreciated.[48]

5

The Judith Plays (1916 and 1919)

The designs Ricketts created for the Irish plays and the way in which the company adapted and transformed the costumes from one character to another arose naturally out of the ensemble pattern of acting for which the Abbey players were famous. The success of these designs and the considerable creative effort represented by their flexibility suggest that this type of production was very close to Ricketts' heart. It would appear to be a concept he shared with William Morris and George Bernard Shaw. The latter, writing to Ricketts as early as 1907, commends this

> most valuable and fascinating stage convention. William Morris used always to say that plays should be performed by four people in conventional costumes, the villain in a red cloak, the father in a bob-wig, etc., etc., etc., etc., and I have always loved Harlequin, Columbine, Sganarelle, etc. in eighteenth century Italian Comedy and French champetre painting. If only we could get a few plays with invisible backgrounds and lovely costumes like that in a suitable theatre.... [1]

Much as Ricketts approved of the use of adaptable costumes for ensemble acting he was also familiar with the more commercial theatre tradition associated with star performers. Throughout the eighteenth and nineteenth centuries, though there were isolated attempts at visual unity of presentation, it was common for actors to simply wear "found" costumes. This system seems very haphazard and no doubt created unintentionally amusing results from time to time, but on the whole it must have worked fairly well as the actor-managers, the only players financially capable of personal lavishness in costume, would, in their managerial capacities, have taken some care for the overall visual effect of the *mis-en-scène*. This method of costuming continued, to some extent, into the twentieth century and was particularly the case for charity productions, which were very popular with celebrated actresses during the Great War. [2]

Retrogressive as this system of costuming would have seemed to someone with Ricketts' concern for the total visual control of sets, costumes, properties and lighting, he did acquiesce in it, at least in the case of his close friend, Lillah McCarthy. For example, he designed her Lady Mary's desert island costume from J.M. Barrie's *The Admirable Crichton* and her Annajanska uniform for Shaw's play of that name, though he did not design either of these productions in its entirety.[3]

Lillah McCarthy and Ricketts had been close friends since 1908 when he designed the Don Juan in Hell episode from Shaw's *Man and Superman* in which she played Dona Ana. Apart from Gabrielle Enthoven, Mary Davis, Katherine Bradley and Edith Cooper (the Michael Fields), the Princess of Monaco, and Maria Appia (Mrs. Sturge Moore), Ricketts had few close female friends.[4] Yet his sudden friendship with Lillah McCarthy was as permanent as it was surprising. The literary style of her autobiography, *Myself and My Friends,* demonstrates a flamboyance and impulsiveness seemingly incompatible with the ascetic refinement of Ricketts.[5] Perhaps he took to her because they shared many of the same ideas about theatre and because she was, in her own way, as much of a pioneer of the new drama as was he.

Trained in Shakespearian acting with William Poel and in the old, touring repertory tradition with such actor-managers as Wilson Barrett and Ben Greet, Lillah McCarthy was already an accomplished and seasoned actress when she joined Harley Granville Barker at the Court Theatre in the early years of the twentieth century.[6] Lillah McCarthy created the role of Ann Whitefield in Shaw's *Man and Superman* at the Court Theatre in 1905 and appeared in many other Barker productions at the Court. After Barker withdrew from the stage, Lillah McCarthy continued as an actress and theatrical manager on her own. Besides her physical beauty, she had, by all accounts, considerable emotional range and a mellifluous, powerful voice. Increasingly she devoted herself to the art of verse speaking, to the promotion of the new poetical drama and to the revival of interest in productions of the Greek classics. As an actress she is particularly famous for her portrayal of such tragic heroines as Jocasta, Hecuba and Iphigenia in the Gilbert Murray verse translations of Sophocles and Euripides.

Lillah McCarthy and Ricketts had many friends and colleagues in common, not least of whom was George Bernard Shaw whose work had first brought them together. Some concept of their mutual understanding can be gathered from the actress's statement:

> Charles Ricketts understands [an actress's needs]—all his letters show it. He knows that the part which the actress plays is a dual part: a duet between herself and the clothes she wears, and that if her clothes are out of harmony, the result is discord and not music.[7]

And her comment upon the very last design Ricketts created for her, the dress she wore in the Sarah Siddons centennial celebrations in 1931:

> a wonderful costume which I wore when in a play celebrating Sarah Siddons, I represented that immortal actress playing Lady Macbeth in the sleepwalking scene. It was one of the most wonderful of all his productions. Those who have the artistic temperament will know

that I do not exaggerate when I say that the wearing of that dress helped me to convey the tragedy, the horror and the pity which that scene evokes.[8]

Few designers could resist such admiration, especially coming from a famous beauty, and Ricketts, despite his natural reserve, responded to McCarthy's enthusiasm. Her biography, though written when she was already a relatively mature woman, unintentionally reveals that beneath her surface bravura lay the impressionable character of a young girl. To comprehend this aspect of her nature one need only reflect upon some of the men she most admired—George Bernard Shaw, H.G. Wells, Arnold Bennett, Charles Ricketts—all noted teachers and doctrinarians. Throughout their long friendship Ricketts would send her letters, postcards, telegrams and notes praising her work. Such of these communications as still exist remind one of Shaw's messages to actresses, in that along with any commendation there would inevitably be some advice, some little lesson on how to improve. For example, the postscript to a letter praising her playing in a charity performance of Alfred de Musset's *A Door Must be Open or Shut* recommends:

> Keep hair very sleek and slightly over cheek. Very white make-up and white hands, as yellow tends to redden and darken the complexion. The carriage of the hands and pocket-handkerchief was greatly studied in those days, and the hands sometimes clasped in front over handkerchief. Early portraits of Queen Victoria give this. The carriage of the head and neck were also studied and very circular. *Today* all the movements of women are too abrupt and too rapid, and not *gracious* enough.[9]

We gather something of the open-minded modesty of this famous actress from the fact that she not only accepted such advice but relished and preserved these letters, which a lesser actress might have taken as a designer's interference.

Lillah McCarthy was certainly one of the most celebrated actresses of her day. If the lasting impression of her has not been so great as of some of her contemporaries, perhaps this is because no major contemporary dramatist succeeded in creating roles for her which made the most of her specific talents. Even the memory of her parts in Shaw's plays is somewhat eclipsed by the fame of his later leading ladies, Mrs. Patrick Campbell and Sybil Thorndike.[10] Though Lillah McCarthy made a considerable contribution to the success of John Masefield's *The Tragedy of Nan,* this play, like most poetic dramas of this period, had at best a limited and specialized kind of attainment. Two particular examples of this failure to create memorable roles for Lillah McCarthy can be studied in the two Judith plays in both of which she played the lead, and both of which Ricketts designed. Thomas Sturge Moore's one-act verse drama *Judith* was produced by the Incorporated Stage Society at the Queen's Theatre in January 1916. Three years later in April 1919, Arnold Bennett's three-act prose *Judith* was produced by Lillah McCarthy at the Kingsway Theatre, London, after brief runs in Eastbourne and Manchester.[11]

The Apocryphal story of Judith of Bethulia seems, at first glance, to be made for dramatization. Bethulia, a city of Judea, is besieged by the Assyrians under the command of Holofernes. The sheltered widow, Judith, saves the city and its endangered faith by descending into the Assyrian camp, seducing Holofernes and beheading him in his sleep. Without much difficulty the story could be made very appropriate to times of war, dealing as it does with a state of siege, with assuming a heroic personal morality in face of foreign aggression, with undertaking a repulsive duty for the sake of preserving racial values. Unfortunately, it is also possible to see Holofernes as the weak but innocent victim of a cheap trick, and this is a tendency of sympathy which neither of these plays does very much to redress.

T. Sturge Moore's verse play, *Judith,* like many early twentieth-century poetic dramas, runs the risk of sounding like third-rate Shakespeare, for example:

> What! What!
> The Melon? Devilled imp!
> The paunched child hath sneaked away with it.[12]

The prose version by Arnold Bennett avoids this trap only to fall into the more obvious one of sounding quasi-Biblical, for example:

> Great prince, receive the words of your servant and suffer your handmaid to speak in your presence, and I will declare no lie to my lord.[13]

Such literary contortions only serve to remove the action from the audience. Unfortunately the basic facts of the plot are also relatively static. The only real action consists of the seduction followed by the murder. Yet, to avoid the ludicrous, the beheading of Holofernes has to be carried out offstage, or else obscured in some way from the eyes of the audience. Sturge Moore no doubt remembered the Literary Theatre Society's 1906 production of Wilde's *Salome* with its similar problem of aesthetic distancing, and Arnold Bennett had certainly enough experience of theatre to avoid this pitfall.[14] Both plays effectively obscure this part of the action, which, however, inevitably makes both plots even more static. Of course, Greek classical drama, to cite only the most obvious case, provides many examples of bloody deeds performed offstage which, nevertheless, lend a sense of scale, of tragic grandeur. Neither of the Judith plays under discussion achieves this effect. Both plays remain remote, wooden, earthbound. This, in turn, puts a greater burden on the designer to provide at least some visual interest.

Throughout his life Thomas Sturge Moore venerated Charles Ricketts and regarded him as his aesthetic mentor. Ricketts encouraged Moore in his various artistic endeavors, and they often worked in collaboration. Moore had worked with Ricketts at the Vale Press and throughout his life continued to design books, bindings and typographic illustrations under the influence of Ricketts' early achievements in this field. His poetry and verse dramas were never widely popular, though they are now acquiring some critical interest.[15] The friendship between the two men was increased, if anything, after Moore's marriage to Maria Appia, the niece of Adolphe Appia, the influential design theorist.[16] She brought a Continental flavor to the Ricketts circle, which Ricketts greatly appreciated. Ricketts had designed Moore's first play *Aphrodite against Artemis* in 1906, but not his own part in the production, nor their friendship, nor the protective care of the Michael Fields, who nurtured the fledgling poet's essay into dramatic verse, could prevent Ricketts' unfeigned enjoyment of the production's ludicrous failure. An unpublished letter from Ricketts to the Michael Fields chides their defensive attitude to the play, and continues:

> During the performance I nearly died with laughter, and both Theseus and Hippolytus have since banished themselves to the provinces out of sorrow.... Please ponder over these events and realise how tragic it would have been had I died on Sunday with a pocket handkerchief stuck down my mouth, with the coroner's verdict, "Found dead by strangulation whilst in a sound frame of mind."[17]

The young poet's feelings were obviously not permanently damaged by Ricketts' laughter for they continued to work so closely together that, during the preliminary discussions leading up to the production of *Judith,* we find Ricketts far exceeding a designer's normal function and suggesting textual improvements:

> Dear Moore,
>   This is only a *suggestion.* Why not let one negro only enter the tent and the others file off immediately. Then make them return (possibly with Bagoas) holding fruit and wine etc. after the exit of Mira, after the line
> "By Jacob's God at midnight,"
> this would lead to the line
> "Send forth thy slaves."
> Judith could then take the cup from one of them. I feel this suggestion would give more movement to scenes, and give stage point to the lines, and save an awkward movement or two when slaves file in and out of tent. I have told Adams I have made this suggestion to you but don't use it if you don't like it.
>   With regard to canopy, there is *no* difficulty, the huge thing I made rolls up in a second without difficulty into a bundle the size of a large pair of books. I had not realised this, it can be reduced in size at rehearsal if necessary. I have added pearls and emeralds to it and see no technical difficulties in its use.[18]

Ricketts' criticisms seem very logical, yet the published text does not incorporate his suggestions, so Moore may have ignored them. A further letter from Ricketts to Moore discusses the production costs. This letter includes a rough thumbnail sketch for the set:

My Dear Moore,

I have designed the dresses and scene for *Judith.* I have done my utmost to keep down cost, giving most of the people bare feet and dressing them in shirts, gowns, loincloths, tabards etc. but I fear, as usual that something extra may cost money. Could you come to grub on Friday at *seven* and tell me how things stand, cast, date of production and who undertakes execution of dresses, props, etc.

My belief, based on Mrs. Champion's estimates for Yeats and Barker plays is that the dresses will average 30 shillings and £2 apiece, with say a pound or so more for Judith and Holofernes. I have constructed scene with I imagine twenty-yards of scrim or canvas and a sort of column of the type we used in *The Persians,* which cost 30 bob, I mean the column. Remains an iron hoop, a couch and some cords, etc.—it is always the etc. that costs. I imagine the thing should cost between £20 and £25 but one never knows. The Haymarket Theatre has or had a good starlight sky made under my directions for Shaw's *Lady of the Sonnets.* I could do some of the stencilling myself. The block man, i.e. the man who can block materials is free on Monday to undertake the work during the week. I fancy Burnett's has still the stuffs I have in view, there is a famine of materials however, owing to War, some colours being unobtainable, blues, violets, certain reds.[19]

The design for this setting is now in the private collection of Carl Woodring, New York. It follows the lines described in Ricketts' letter. Against the dark background of a starlit sky, and set off to one side of the stage, stands a great circular tent about three times the height of a human figure. Folds of draperies fall from a hoop suspended near the top of the sight-lines. On top of the hoop there is a low-pitched roof to the tent made of the same drapery material as the sides. A front opening is created by simply pulling the side panels of the tent back so that one can see into the interior. There is a low pile of mattresses and pillows forming a couch. Within the tent a great banner or canopy gleams above the couch creating an effect of luxury and decadence. To one side stands a high pillar set exactly before the moon, so that the primitive war helmet which crowns the post is a constant reminder of Judith's purpose and of the desperate straits of her people. The harshness of the pillar of war set against the soft flowing lines of the tent forms such a simplified yet complete visual statement of the theme of the play that one is reminded of Yeatsian dramatic symbolism.[20] However, the friendship and communications between Yeats and Ricketts, Ricketts and Moore, Moore and Yeats are too considerable to be able to attribute specific influence to or from any one of the three.

As Ricketts' letter indicates, the set would be relatively inexpensive, especially if the backdrop could be borrowed. In terms of composition the design is classical, pleasing, chaste. He also achieves great depth of field, so that the sides of the tent appear to recede back to the night sky as far as the eye can see, giving great scale to the two free-standing structures. The tent is a silvery

eau de Nil color with a lavender pattern. The inside of the tent is black, except
for the great gold-patterned canopy. The pillar is blood red with touches of dull
green. Artistic license is taken in that the moon appears in the sky at some
distance behind the foreground, yet the stage is cut by a shaft of moonlight
shining across the front of the stage and illuminating at least part of the interior
of the tent. The text also indicates that Bagoas has a lamp and tinder box, and
that the six Negro slaves carry silver lamps which could be used to "cheat" as
potential light sources at such times as the inside of the tent needs to be clearly
visible.

The only design which we can attribute with any certainty to this, rather
than the later play, is for one of Judith's costumes, also in the collection of Carl
Woodring. A production photograph of Lillah McCarthy wearing this dress
and playing on a psaltery appeared in *The Tatler* at the time of the production
(fig. 23). For her first entrance she would also have had a dark cloak concealing
her brighter clothes. The costume consists of loose black pants gathered at the
ankles into bands of yellow material, covered by a free-flowing tabard in
emerald and white. This garment is open at the sides, slashed in a deep V-shape
at the front and has a long train at the back. Over it there is a short, curved skirt,
in a checkered pattern of the same colors, worn completely open at the front. A
large golden brooch holds together the deep neckline. The principal garment is
a large semicircular shawl which is loosely thrown over the shoulders and falls
to the ground where heavy tassels weigh it down. Colored a pale yellow with a
stenciled design of big black roses in the art nouveau style, it complements the
tightly patterned whites, blue and greens of the undergarments. The headdress
is a bright blue pointed cap held in place with bands of gold and with twisted
gold decorations over the ears. The loose-fitting hair mingles with streamers
falling from the cap, some of which are of the same blue material, others of
which are a dull gold with a white peacock's eye design further adorned with
dark green beads. The general feeling is loose and sensuous, yet the costume is
entirely modest. The *Tatler* photograph shows the complete dress as a faithful
execution of the design, with the one difference that the materials used have a
stiffness which Ricketts probably did not intend, presumably brought about by
considerations of economy.

The harp or psaltery in the photograph is not required in the text, but it
throws some light on Moore's reservations in the following letter of thanks to
Ricketts. It should be explained that, to some extent promoted by Yeats, the
lyre or psaltery experienced a certain vogue in the theatrical productions of this
period. Various theories of chanting verse to musical notations accompanied
by rudimentary instruments were encouraged by such diverse characters as
Florence Farr, Edmund Dulac and Arnold Dolmetsch, sometimes working
together but not always with the same ends in view.[21] Decidedly unmusical and
often unintelligible results were not infrequent.[22] Photogenic possibilities and
usefulness in striking histrionic poses, rather than musical potential, seem to

Figure 23.   Thomas Sturge Moore's *Judith*: Judith
               *(Courtesy Enthoven Collection, Victoria and Albert
               Museum)*

have been largely responsible for the psaltery's popularity. Towards the end of his life Dolmetsch admitted that not even Yeats, with all his enthusiasm, could recite to the tones of the instrument:

> I tried to revive the art of reciting to well defined musical tones, and I made a "Psaltery" to accompany the voice, as was done in the early days of Celtic and Greek Art.... I spent a whole night listening to Yeats reciting but ... he had a short phrase of fairly indistinct tones which he employed to recite any of his poems. This did not interfere with the expression of his readings, which were beautiful; but it was useless from my point of view.[23]

In this particular production of *Judith* these experiments must have been pressed into service for that strange moment in the play when Judith, behind the closed flaps of the tent, is possessed of enough heavenly strength to sever Holofernes' head. Moore, in what is a decidedly prosaic suggestion for a poet, indicates that Judith's inspiration may take the form of a young male angel:

> *Judith suddenly from within the tent in an altered voice as though possessed by an angel.* (To ensure this effect if there is any room for doubt these lines should be spoken by a young man). [II, 149]

Ricketts' comprehension of music was, perhaps, finer than that possessed by most of the experimenters.[24] He counseled Moore to drop the whole thing but to no avail:

> Dear Ricketts,
>   I must write to thank you for the magnificent picture that *Judith* made on the stage, and all the pains you so lavishly expended on what from some other sides was, alas! being carelessly botched together.... I must confess that I think it was a tactical mistake to persuade Lillah to change from the chanting at such short notice. What replaced it was not, I think, so good.
>   Of course, she ought never to have chanted in the tent when Mira calls from the outside, but she seemed unable to get any effect and even suggested saying the words to some cry, used from Mosques in Cairo.... And so I went to Dolmetsch again. I did not realize that you meant that all the chanting should be dropped even when the stage directions give a song....
>   Dolmetsch ... at least does save both words and rhythm.... However the songs and their delivery whether bad or good can be given too much importance in regard to the whole. Lillah certainly surpassed herself ... and of course was enhanced a thousand-fold by your dress.[25]

Another letter, from Maria, Moore's wife, adds another compliment to the designer. In the circumstances one must assume that she is innocent of any intentional irony:

> Vous seul pouviez faire parler et chanter les étoffes et les couleurs comme un orchestre magnifique se mêlant au poème pour l'enricher et le compléter.[26]

Problems with the verse notwithstanding, the production was obviously a visually stimulating experience, and Lillah McCarthy's interest in dramatizing the tale of Judith remaining unsatisfied, Ricketts had a second opportunity to design a version of the story. Two years later we find that the actress has persuaded Arnold Bennett to write another *Judith*. Bennett's journal for 10 December 1918 reads:

> Week-end at Dr. F. Keeble's at Weybridge. Lillah McCarthy also there.... I promised to write her a play on the subject of Judith, if a firm contract was made at once.[27]

Until very recently Bennett's critical star even as a novelist has been in decline, and we tend to forget the very considerable stature he once held in literary circles. Besides the popularity and critical acclaim of his novels and essays, he was highly successful financially and socially, the very image of the man self-made through the careful marketing of his literary products. Like many novelists of his epoch he was fascinated by the theatre and spent much of his spare time in the company of actors. He wrote several plays and film scenarios and interested himself in theatrical production. At the very time Lillah McCarthy approached him about writing *Judith* he was cofounding the now famous period at the Lyric Theatre, Hammersmith. He was joint director with Nigel Playfair and Alistair Tayler for the first seven years of this new venture, which took theatrical London by surprise in proving that long runs were possible, beyond the tiny orbit of established west-end theatres, provided that the theatrical event was worth the journey. The Lyric had a number of very long runs of interesting new plays and revivals of eighteenth-century comedies; Drinkwater's *Abraham Lincoln,* Congreve's *The Way of the World* and, most famous of all, Gay's *The Beggar's Opera* with the delightful, modified-historical designs of Claude Lovat Fraser.[28] It is often forgotten that this much praised production used Gay's text brilliantly edited and distilled by Arnold Bennett. Inevitably, Bennett also brought a sound business acumen to any theatrical production with which he was connected.

Lillah McCarthy's instinct in approaching Bennett would seem to have been right-headed. He certainly threw himself into the concept: "I finished *Judith* yesterday at 7:30 having written it in twenty-three days."[29] The actress-manager had reservations about the text:

> I began reading it with eagerness, but finished it with disappointment. Bennett's treatment of the Judith story seemed to me, and still seems, superb. The tent scene... is charged with drama. But Bennett had not been content to let the Apocryphal story alone. He wove into it another, a romance. Brought in love to soften the terrible asperities of hate, and failed to bring the two motives into dramatic irony. Though I felt sure my judgement was right, I stood too much in awe of Bennett to tell him what I thought.[30]

The play opened early in April 1919 at the Devonshire Park Theatre in Eastbourne. Bennett's journal describes the excitement of the opening night, Lillah's rather high-handed behavior in her dual capacity as star and manager, the reactions of the actors:

> She [Lillah McCarthy] protested that all the creative producing work had been done by me, M. [Marguerite, his wife] and her.... Ernest Thesiger, the Bagoas, grew sterner as the hour of performance came nearer. I don't think he smiled on Monday at all. He is really an artist. He gave a magnificent performance. Esme Hubbard (Haggith) remained light and merry throughout, and gave a magnificent performance. Frederick Volpe (Ingur) behaved rather like Thesiger and was very fine.[31]

Bennett's excitement and critical interest survived as long as the London opening at the Kingsway Theatre. His journal notes the house returns were the highest ever taken at any first night in that theatre. Unfortunately Lillah's first reactions on reading the script were borne out in the confused response from critics and public alike. On May 14 Bennett writes:

> Receipts for first complete week of *Judith* just under £900—too much psychological realism in play to please a large section of the public. On Monday night the receipts fell to £56.... We know after this the play must be regarded as a failure.[32]

It is not so much psychological realism that spoils the play but the uneasy mixture of heroism, low comedy and satire, while a number of themes are left ill-defined. Thomas Hardy, whose own play *The Dynasts* at the same theatre had had an even poorer reception, was reported to be enthusiastic about *Judith*.[33] One can only imagine that he responded to one of its underdeveloped themes, that expressed in Haggith's retort when reproved for eating unsanctified, alien food:

> For such as my high-born mistress, it is an offence. But for the handmaid—pooh! She eats as she can, and the Lord turneth away his glance.... —[pp. 80-81]

On a minute scale this remark echoes Hardy's own treatise in *The Dynasts*.

Bennett's play, though often well written, darts about in too many directions to make it a satisfactory theatrical experience. Perhaps Lillah McCarthy best expresses the basic cause of the play's failure when she writes:

> I understand something of the mood of a people at war. Hardy's *Dynasts* and John Masefield's *Philip the Second,* both of which tell of heroic moments in our history, fell on deaf ears. The drama of the present so obsessed all minds that they had no room for the drama of past times.[34]

In any case, heroic, as separate from tragic, drama is a notoriously difficult form. Bennett's play aggravates this difficulty by surrounding the heroism with subplots and secondary themes. One element that might sell a heroic drama in times of national hardship is the possibility of some exotic element in the design. Ricketts supplied this element to the extent that his budget would allow. No serious drama however can succeed on design alone, if its meaning is otherwise diffuse, and for sheer exotic fantasy on a truly lavish scale, without the inconvenience of ideas, the public could always turn to a pantomime like *Chu Chin Chow,* already in its third year at His Majesty's Theatre when Bennett's *Judith* was produced.[35] As Lillah McCarthy expressed it in retrospect:

> I can see now that whoever had written it [*Judith*] at that time, and no matter how it had been written, the play would still have failed.... The instincts of people living under a great shadow are to seek diversion and entertainment.[36]

Though Ricketts probably knew the play's success would be limited, he threw himself into the designing of this piece for his old friend's venture into theatrical management. Such designs as exist reveal the designer at the height of his powers. He made finished presentation copies of several of the designs and gave them to his friends. Fortunately a number of these are now in public or accessible private galleries, and they can be compared to a group of production photographs now in the Enthoven Collection at the Victoria and Albert Museum.[37] There are also ten very rough costume sketches in the Harvard Theatre Collection.

Only one working drawing of one of the sets exists in any form, a rather poor photograph at the Witt Collection of the Courtauld Institute, London. The set requirements for the play are a street scene in Bethulia, the valley near the Assyrian camp, the interior of Holofernes' tent, and a return to the first set. Other changes can be indicated by lighting. The photograph in the Witt Library shows the first setting. The set has been described by Lillah McCarthy:

> The first scene was surely one of the most beautiful ever designed—it showed the great bronze gates and towers of a besieged city, and when you looked upon it hunger could be seen stalking the streets.[38]

The gate is positioned far downstage and off to one side. It forms a focal point for much of the action, as Judith exits from it in some trepidation in Act I and returns through it crowned with victory and surrounded by cheering citizens in Act III. The city walls also provide the opportunity for some slight indication of a tent or shade to represent the elevated dwelling and vantage point where Judith has formerly secluded herself in widowhood. By positioning this whole first set at an angle, so that it seems like some corner of a monumental citadel, Ricketts not only achieves a sense of great scale but also prepares the way for very quick changes to the other two sets. Unfortunately no evidence of these other designs exists but it would seem fairly obvious that the second set was a flat rolled backdrop or traverse which falls in front of the first set. All that is required is some painted representation of a great valley with Bethulia on a hill in the far distance. This backdrop or curtain could then be removed to reveal the interior of Holofernes' tent which is most likely to have been a semicircle of draperies dropped in front of the first, triangular set. Variety could be introduced to this semicircular tent shape by hanging various rugs, trophies of war, banners, cords and some additional curtains to screen the couch and the entrances to the tent. All of this third set could be rolled up or pulled aside very quickly even in the most primitive of theatres, leaving only the couch, some cushions and a low table to be moved off to return to the original street scene. The semicircular or concave arrangement of curtains was a particular favorite of Ricketts; indeed he claimed to have originated its theatrical use.[39] Given his love and knowledge of the East, one can readily imagine that he would have created a most rich and evocative scene.[40]

No design exists for the costume of Ozias, the vain and lecherous governor of Bethulia, but there is a production photograph. The main feature of the stenciled tunic is the use of tiers of colored fringes swaying in deep curves across the garment and gathered at the shoulder from whence they cascade down one side. Echoing this movement in the costume are several strands of heavy beads. With this he wears the pointed cap with a contrasting edge that Ricketts gives to most of the Judeans.

The design for Judith's maid, Haggith, seems to have been modified in its execution (figs. 24 and 25). I imagine this would have been because the actress Esme Hubbard who played the part was a mere girl. Her movements would have been terribly hampered by the voluminous folds of the original design, especially since she has a considerable amount of fetching and carrying to perform. The production photograph shows far less bulk around the arms, feet and waist, and the blue fringe which had originally been around the shoulders now surrounds the hips, giving more of a womanly outline to a scarcely nubile figure. Young as she is, the actress who plays Haggith must suggest femininity to fit the character of the rather knowing wench who subjects the Assyrian soldier, Ingur. It is typical of Ricketts that, to help the young actress, he has supplied a hand prop, not demanded by the text, which appears to be a scrolled map of the Assyrian camp.

Much of the action in Act I and in Act II, scene i involves the maid in close relation to her mistress, the widow Judith. No design exists for Judith's first costume but we get some impression of it from the production photograph (fig. 29) and from Lillah McCarthy's own description:

> My dress...in that City of Sorrows was composed of every tone of black: brown black, green black, blue and grey black: folded one over the other.[41]

These muted tones of translucent black veils must have made a pleasing contrast with the clear blue, white and green with touches of terra cotta and

Figure 24.   Arnold Bennett's *Judith*: [Judith's Maid]
(Courtesy Ashmolean Museum, Oxford)

Figure 25.   Arnold Bennett's *Judith*: Judith's Maid (photograph)
               (Courtesy Enthoven Collection, Victoria and Albert
               Museum)

gold which make up Haggith's costume. The widow's dress is completed by a high, peaked headdress which completely conceals the neck and hair. It is outlined with yards of soft white material which binds the head, drapes in a deep curve to the waist, and then again in a deeper curve draped almost to the floor, then up again to the right wrist.

The central figure in the group photograph is Achior, the young Assyrian captain whom Judith saves from punishment. His costume is distinguished by its deep leather belt with multiple buckles, by its pointed helmet and by the type of sandal he wears. Some concept of the difference between the Assyrian and the Israelite soldiers can also be gathered from the group photograph (fig. 29).

In Act II, scene i there has to be some slight change in Judith's costume because at one point in this scene she is *"elaborately veiled in a series of veils by Bagoas and his attendants"* while on stage. It would be manifestly ridiculous to add any more veils on top of her widow's weeds, so there has to be a change of costume before this. The major transformation in her dress, however, takes place in the tent scene, Act II, scene ii. Two versions of the design for this costume exist, each showing a slightly different pose: one in the City Art Gallery at Derby, the other sold privately by The Fine Art Society, London, a few years ago (fig. 26). The Fine Art Society version is the later of the two, as a thin band of black velvet has been added to secure the lower section to the tight band which binds the breasts. It is perhaps difficult for us to realize quite how adventurous this costume was for a "legitimate" actress on a public stage, rather than in a private society or club theatre, in 1919. Arnold Bennett's doubts are expressed in his journals. Of the opening night at Eastbourne he wrote:

> Her tent costume frightened one of the lessees of the theatre. Above a line drawn about 1/2 inch or 1 inch about [above?] the "mont de Venus," she wore nothing except a 5 in. band of black velvet round the body hiding the breasts and a similar perpendicular band of velvet starting from between the breasts and going down to the skirt and so hiding the navel. Two thin shoulder straps held this contrivance in position. Bracelets and rings, of course. The skirt was slit everywhere and showed the legs up to the top of the thigh, when she lay down there at Holofernes' feet. She looked a magnificent picture thus, but a police prosecution would not have surprised me at all.

and of the London opening:

> I never before took so much interest in the production of a play of mine. *Judith* was produced at the Kingsway Theatre, London, last Wednesday, 30th April. . . . In the Second Act Lillah McCarthy had put down her dress as low as it was at the first night at Eastbourne (after raising it for later performances at Eastbourne, and for dress rehearsals in London).[42]

Perhaps the addition of the vertical black band and the raising of the skirt portion had something to do with appeasing public morality but I suggest it also helped to hold the costume together. There are so many flying panels and

Figure 26.   Arnold Bennett's *Judith*: Judith (modified costume)
(Courtesy Fine Art Society, London)

beaded decorations hanging from the skirt that it would have been in considerable danger of dropping off had it not been attached to the tight breast-covering with its thin shoulder straps. The open skirt is blue with a white pattern and green fringes. From the black velvet band at the hips hang long trailing sections, yellow with a black chevron pattern. The shoulders are covered by a large yellow wrap bearing a squared black motif. A flimsy red scarf is tucked in at the dropped waist, and this same color is repeated in the many strings of beads, the bracelets and tassels. In the earlier design, Judith is barefoot; in the later version sandals have been added, giving the actress a little more height. The peaked headdress has the usual Judean contrasting band, only in this instance it is studded with jewels. The ears are covered by swaying, fan-shaped decorations. In the earlier design she holds what is obviously the murder weapon. Several of the production photographs show the completed costume. As with several of the costumes in the production there is a stiffness in the painted or stenciled fabrics which is difficult to avoid when using this kind of decorative technique, but the completed dress still has that strange combination of sensuality and dignity demanded by the role.

After the murder of Holofernes, Judith returns in triumph to her city. A reproduction of the design for her robe of victory is published in *Charles Ricketts, R.A., Sixty-Five Illustrations.*[43] A clearer image of the costume can be seen in the close-up photograph (fig. 27). The garment is a great double cape. The first layer falls to a train at the sides and back. The top layer is grasped loosely around the arms and shoulders. On top of the previous headdress she wears a victor's wreath. The close-up photograph (fig. 27) gives an indication of the intricate care Ricketts took with jewelry. It also gives a clear picture of the stenciled patterns, a mixture of stylized flowers and strange asymmetrical shapes. One can almost feel the thick ridge of paint at the edge of each pattern, and appreciate the great difficulty of using this method to decorate any light-weight material. In the case of this cape, weight is not an important consideration and the patterns sit well upon the material.

The design for Bagoas presents some difficulty. A transparency of a design with the name "Bagoes" in Ricketts' handwriting is one of a group of reproductions in the files of the University of Bristol Department of Drama Library. The original source of the reproduction is unknown. It is catalogued as "Arnold Bennett's *Judith* (1916) Ernest Thesiger." The date, of course, is wrong, being confused with the earlier play, in which Bagoas was played by Andrew Leigh. A further problem is presented by the set of five designs offered for sale recently by the Fine Art Society, London, all of which are untitled but one of which is the Judith costume already discussed (fig. 26). It can safely be assumed that all five of these designs, probably originally from the estate of the Dowager Princess of Monaco, Ricketts' old friend, are for Arnold Bennett's *Judith.* The one male design in the set seems to epitomize the popular image of a eunuch. The only other figure he could possibly represent is one of the elders

Figure 27.   Arnold Bennett's *Judith*: Judith (close-up)
(Courtesy Enthoven Collection, Victoria and Albert Museum)

of Bethulia, but he looks altogether too well-fed to be a citizen of that ravished city. I can only suggest that Ricketts designed this costume for the eunuch, Bagoas, before Lillah McCarthy had settled on Thesiger for the role, and that he worked on the assumption that the eunuch would be some stout actor. He could be forgiven for this concept, for there are a number of references to Bagoas' size and laziness in the text, for example:

Holofernes. Thou wilt go thyself to fetch them, elephant. [p. 83]

Apparently Lillah McCarthy cast well, as Thesiger was excellent in the role and went on to create a number of similar parts, most notably the waspy, effete dauphin in Shaw's *Saint Joan.* If my hypothesis is correct, Ricketts would then have made a completely new design for a Bagoas of a different shape. The fact that the reproduction of the design in the University of Bristol files is rather different from the completed costume of the production photograph could be explained in a number of ways; possibly the costumes were already under construction and the fabrics blocked and something had to be put together with what remained. Whatever the reasons for this disparity, the photograph of the completed costume shows a most bizarre figure with tiered skirts in boldly contrasting patterns, a deep fringe worn over one shoulder and a strange pointed cap worn over a Balaclava-type helmet. It is certainly a study in misplaced but obsessive vanity. The pose indicates a mincing gate which would make the tiered, fringed concoction all the more ridiculous in movement.

I was, at first, confused by the costume labeled Jewish dancer in the Victoria and Albert Museum, till I discovered a production photograph in *Dancing Times* showing the executed design. Bennett does not call for dancers specifically, but Lillah McCarthy must have decided to enliven the triumphal return of Judith in this way. The stage direction at this point simply reads: *"Enter through the gates a procession of women (including Rahel) waving branches"* (p. 117). The caption to the magazine photograph states that the subject, Molly Lake, is the principal dancer, so that there must have been a troupe of dancers. The costume is a heavily patterned red and white wraparound skirt with blue and green fringes, worn with a blue top and a bare midriff. The yellow and green of the headdress are picked up in the many light scarves with bright tassels that fly loosely from waist and shoulders. In the design the dancer beats a tambourine and is shown in a swaying motion so that one can easily imagine the lively impression created by a group of such dancers swirling exultantly through the great bronze gates.

The design for Holofernes, in the City of Leeds Art Gallery (fig. 28), has been faithfully executed in the costume, as shown in the production photographs. The colors are black, gold and blue. Ricketts obviously had in mind a taller, more muscular actor than Claude King, the actor in this case, who does nevertheless succeed in conveying the arrogance indicated by the

Figure 28.   Arnold Bennett's *Judith*: Holofernes
(Courtesy Leeds City Art Gallery)

design. The principal garment is a long wrapped kilt heavily patterned with motifs taken from ancient architectural decoration. There is also a deep belt around the chest, built up from layers of leather, and a similar belt around the waist. The photograph reveals that the pointed, eastern sandals of the design have been replaced by a much simpler leather type, built up in such a way as to give the actor more height. They add a nice touch of vanity. The helmet is notable for its heavy chin piece protecting what is, all too obviously, a false black beard.

Holofernes is surrounded by a number of attendants and concubines, giving the production an extravagant sense of scale. A design in the Victoria and Albert Museum shows the "Attendant on Holofernes," who carries a large pumpkin-colored parasol which has a curious little flap at the back to give further protection. The servant wears a stiff, cone-shaped, fringed skirt with patterns of brown and white on blue and green backgrounds. A brief blue top covers the upper chest and shoulders. The headdress is a bright blue fez with orange feathers and streamers. He wears a great deal of heavy silver jewelry. The costume has a certain resemblance to that of some ancient bull-dancer in the frescoes of Minoan Crete. In the Witt Library there is a tiny photograph of this design plus another for one of the black servants of the tent. The photograph is so small, however, that it does little more than suggest a boldly patterned skirt, a considerable extent of naked flesh and Ricketts' usual concern for elaborate headdresses. Occasionally over the past few years a number of rough sketches, often on postcards, and similar in style to the above design have been offered for sale by the Fine Art Society. They probably relate to this production of *Judith.*

Another three highly finished designs from the set of five (including Judith) offered for sale some years ago by the Fine Arts Society undoubtedly represent some of the silent concubines or tent-women in Bagoas' care. These designs are magnificent watercolors of Eastern costumes and indicate the great trouble Ricketts would take over costumes which are only briefly, and often partially, glimpsed by the audience. The text indicates that these women merely peep from behind the tent hangings from time to time.

Figure 29, which shows Judith, Ozias, one soldier from each camp, and, presumably, one of the old Bethulian citizens, Chabris or Charmis, gives an idea of the effect of all these brightly patterned costumes superimposed one upon the other. By today's standards of high workmanship and comparative extravagance in theatre wardrobes there is something perhaps a little amateurish about the execution of some of these 1919 costumes. Did it really save so much money to use torn strips of fabric for fringes? Did nobody think to press the costumes before the photographer started his work? Did the soldiers' helmets have to look so paper-thin? We should remember that the camera, in the production photographs, was much closer to the costumes than the audience ever would be. The Kingsway was a relatively large house, larger than

Figure 29.   Arnold Bennett's *Judith*: Group Photograph
(*Courtesy Enthoven Collection, Victoria and Albert
Museum*)

the Court Theatre according to Lillah McCarthy, so that the total visual effect may not have been affected by these considerations. Given greater distance than the camera has allowed, the effect might well have been one of bold pattern, sensuous movement and an exotic strangeness of line and color. Even the ragged fringes may have given some pleasing variety of texture.

The Near Eastern location of the two Judith projects, taken together with the *Salome* designs already discussed, inevitably raises the question of Ricketts' place in the history of theatrical design vis-à-vis Léon Bakst, the most famous of a group of designers associated with the *Ballets Russes*.[44] Bakst's most original effects were achieved in his oriental designs, such as *Cleopatra* (1909) and *Schéhérezade* (1910), and his work in this field fascinated audiences in Paris and London from 1909 through 1914. The vogue for realizing Eastern tales upon the stage was not created by any one individual artist. Throughout the nineteenth century Persian and Arabic sources had been an inspiration to many European artists and writers.[45] A major exhibition in Paris of Muslim arts in 1903 increased this interest.

Ricketts was an acknowledged expert on Eastern art and artifacts.[46] Yet his theatrical costumes were never pedantic reconstructions. Generally speaking he tended to simplify line and exaggerate pattern, motif or detail derived from his knowledge of the period and its decorative style. One thinks for example of the stylized lion pattern applied to the relatively simple costume of Holofernes (fig. 28) which captures the three aspects of pride, sovereignty and power found in the character, yet also suggests the East without resorting to painstaking archaeological accuracy. Bakst was not the expert Ricketts was. Bakst's knowledge of the East was most probably derived from late nineteenth-century Russian and French painting. The exact source is rather unimportant since, as Charles Spencer perceives, "he [Bakst] transmuted every influence to the point of elimination."[47] This quality of transmutation makes his inspired improvizations upon oriental lines all the more remarkable.

Ricketts was the most enthusiastic admirer of Bakst and, indeed, of all the Russian Ballet. In one brief season he attended twenty performances.[48] At times, he led the applause against the seeming sluggishness of the British audiences, which would invariably spark off a series of letters or outbursts in his diaries about the Britisher's reluctance to express unguarded delight.[49] When Bakst exhibited his designs and paintings at the Fine Art Society in London in 1912 and 1913, Ricketts is recorded as being one of the purchasers.[50] Later, when subscriptions were sought for an expensive book of Bakst's designs, Ricketts bought a copy and zealously offered to lend it out to his friends.[51] Though, in a postcard to Lillah McCarthy, he jokingly mentions being "sick with jealousy of Bakst & all the dear Russians," the fact that he ends the same card with the injunction "Don't miss *Prince Igor*" indicates that his appreciation was prompted not by envy but by an almost childlike desire to share the things he loved.[52] He is simply overjoyed by this manifestation of a "lambent sense of beauty and desire for perfection" in theatrical art, which, after all, must have made him feel less isolated in his own endeavors.[53]

For all his obvious enthusiasm in recognizing a fellow artist Ricketts was not uncritical, especially in his private correspondence:

> Bakst puts too much detail into all he does, uses too many colours, and hardly husbands his resources. The general effect is often confused and even unpleasant, but he has so much invention and fancy, that one has to accept him on his own terms; he is a brilliant *improvisatore* and has the qualities of his defects. Nature had intended him for a book-illustrator; opportunity, which is a part of genius, has done the rest. I confess that the Russian Ballet, with all its perfection of dancing and beauty of setting, haunts and enchants me like nothing else.... I should like to write about the Russians and the Art of the Theatre—but why bother? To those who like it, nothing need be said. To those who don't, nothing can persuade. There are moments when one would welcome a German invasion if it could cure this country of its listlesness, insincerity, and a wish *not* to believe.[54]

Another letter three years later clarifies the essential difference between his own and Bakst's achievements:

> No, my dear chap, the Russian designers owe me nothing.... My stage-work, which anticipated much of theirs—the all-red *Attila* scene, the all-blue *Salome* and *Lear* tent scene, the all-green *Miracle* scene, and countless details, too long to describe, such as huge patterns and fantastic headdresses, are unknown to them; they [Ricketts' designs] are known here and remembered only by the theatrical profession. Any chance likeness you may detect lies in a common indebtedness to Moreau, or I should say, to things initiated and discovered by Moreau; remains a certain local and semi-Oriental element which is spontaneous, and which, with me, is replaced by many complex currents of experience. Viewing my theatre work in relation to theirs, I should say that theirs is adventurous and lyric, and mine more intimate and always tragic.[55]

The remainder of that part of the letter dealing with the Russians mentions some of the advantages under which the Russian designers worked. One is forced to reflect that Bakst, in his greatest period, worked in association with Benois, another talented designer; with Diaghilev, the great director and impresario; and with a group of talented dancers the like of which had never been gathered together before. By comparison Ricketts never had the opportunity to work for any length of time with one group of players and one director whose talents were equal to his own. Some of his best early designs were created for plays directed by Granville Barker, but, of course, that possibility came to an end when Barker retired from the theatre to the study. At a later date Ricketts did have the chance to work on a number of productions with the Cassons, and these are considered among his major design credits.

One must also remember that the members of the *Ballets Russes* were recruited from the Imperial Russian Theatres, institutions moribund with eighteenth-century French tradition, but nevertheless staffed by an army of trained craftsmen, technicians and artists and supported by the financial resources of an empire on the last heady fling before impending political revolution. Diaghilev, Bakst and Benois made inspired use of these resources, but the resources were there on a scale never imagined in Ricketts' early design projects. Even before the Russian revolution in 1917, Bakst had switched allegiance from Diaghilev and started designing for the émigré heiress Ida Rubinstein. Miss Rubinstein's charms and her series of extremely rich lovers ensured that even after the Revolution there was no lack of money for the creation of Bakst's designs. For her productions, an international galaxy of experts created the sets and costumes from Bakst's designs. Even the rags Rubinstein wore in *La Pisanelle* (1913) were put together by the Paris couturier Worth.[56]

It is essential to separate Bakst's theatrical achievements from his impact upon popular taste. The vogue for exoticism in dress was such that "every woman—and this in the very year of the suffragette demonstrations—was determined to look like a slave in an Oriental harem."[57] The Russian Ballet's effect on interior design and social intercourse was even greater:

> Before one could say Nijinski the pale pastel shades which had reigned supreme...were replaced by a riot of barbaric hues—jade green, purple, every variety of crimson and scarlet, and, above all, orange....The Orient came once more into its own and the piano was draped with Chinese shawls, the divan replaced the chaise-lounge, and no mantlepiece was complete without its Buddha.
>   Not least of the Russian Ballet's achievements was the social kudos it acquired for art...now Art came once more to roost among the duchesses, where it was at length productive of a wave of modified Bohemianism. This produced a tendency to regard a room not so much as a place to live in, but as a setting for a party, with the result that the studio...was suddenly much in demand for purely residential purposes.[58]

As I have already noted Bakst was not the only artist to popularize oriental settings. One need only examine the magnificent book illustrations to *Stories from the Arabian Nights* created in 1907 by Ricketts' friend Edmund Dulac, to imagine how widespread the interest was.[59] Yet Bakst was the catchword for a certain style very loosely based upon Eastern sources, a catchword and a style used and perpetrated by many who had never seen the Russian Ballet.

Charles Spencer concludes his perceptive study of Bakst with the guarded statement:

> That he was the greatest stage designer of the twentieth century is widely accepted. His influence has penetrated in so many diverse ways that it is almost impossible to state them all.[60]

Perhaps it would be more accurate to say that Bakst was the twentieth-century stage-designer whose diverse influence was the greatest. Though his influence was widespread, his achievement was limited. His oriental designs represent him at his best, his most innovative. In other periods, other areas, his work tends to reveal an excessiveness which had been appropriate enough in his Eastern ballet costumes. His sets were often mere pastiche. Bakst's career peaked about 1910 and declined from that point, so that he died in 1924 exhausted from work which never regained the success of his earlier period. Ricketts' *Judith* designs were not his only fine works. His stage career went from strength to strength so that some of his most successful productions were created in the last years of his life. Few people now know Ricketts' name, while one can buy Bakst's designs printed on a bath towel. Ricketts hit upon their essential difference when he said Bakst's designs were "lyric," his own "tragic." By the very nature of their escapist fantasy and sexual license Bakst's designs were bound to reach a greater audience. So much of Ricketts' design work was for new plays by contemporary authors, using difficult dramatic forms, plays which inevitably had a limited appeal. Even those of Ricketts' designs from this period that were realized—and many were not—were unlikely to be seen by great numbers of people. Later he was to reach a larger audience.

6

Saint Joan (1924)

Between Bennett's *Judith* and Shaw's *Saint Joan* Ricketts designed another set of interchangeable costumes for Mrs. Penelope Wheeler's touring company, this time for *Alcestis, Medea* and *Iphigenia in Tauris* (1920), redesigned Wilde's *Salome* for the Shōchiku Company, Tokyo (1919) and created new designs for the opera *Nāïl* composed by his friend Isidore de Lara for Covent Garden (1919) and for Granville Barker, in his last engagement as a director, Maeterlinck's *The Betrothal* at the Gaiety Theatre (1921).[1] I have already discussed the *Salome* designs, little evidence remains concerning the touring production of the Greek plays and nothing can be learned about the opera, except that it was musically dull and was performed only twice.

The *Betrothal*, which is Maeterlinck's last play and forms a sequel to *The Blue Bird*, is a strange mixture of symbolism and pantomime. It was a major production with lots of publicity, starring Gladys Cooper and a cast of over ninety actors. Ricketts' journals and letters leave us in no doubt that he disliked both the play and the popular reaction to it. Certainly he would not have touched it but for the opportunity it provided to work once more with Barker. It was an immense undertaking for one man, the kind of project that in today's theatre would engage a team of designers. The Witt Library at the Courtauld Institute contains many tiny black-and-white photographs of rough sketches for the costumes, and the Ashmolean Museum, Oxford contains a highly finished set design for one scene of the play, in the Palace of the Unborn Children (discussed below, p. 142). The production was withdrawn, after playing for three months to full houses, because the Gaiety Theatre was booked for another show. No other theatre large enough could be found to which *The Betrothal* might be transferred.

Generally speaking these were unrewarding years for Ricketts as far as his reputation as a stage-designer was concerned. The public apathy, with one or two exceptions, to his part in the production of *The Betrothal* was enough to make him give up stage design for three years. He expresses his weariness with the situation in a letter to his young friend Cecil Lewis:

There was a fairly solid body of opinion that nothing quite so beautiful had ever been seen upon the English stage.... For five days Barker and I did not have a square meal and I used to walk home from the theatre between 11 and 12. Was it worthwhile? I can send you nothing that illustrates the play. On the Continent every newspaper would have reproduced my drawings. Here, saving an American ladies paper, the press only brought out large faces of Gladys Cooper; she was the veiled figure.[2]

To some extent his part in the production was recognized, in that the management of the Gaiety Theatre offered him further design work, which he refused. In fact, except when working directly with friends such as Granville Barker, or on charity productions, Ricketts always turned down design offers when he felt out of sympathy with the material. It was the coming together of his two old friends George Bernard Shaw and Lewis Casson, together with Casson's wife, Sybil Thorndike, that brought Ricketts back to stage design in 1924. If he felt that his stage work had not been greatly appreciated till then, he could no longer complain of public neglect after *Saint Joan.* From this time on his designs were always eagerly awaited and given extensive coverage even in the tardy British newspapers and journals.

Ricketts had worked with Lewis Casson on Wilde's *Salome* eighteen years earlier. He had previously designed a number of productions for Shaw: the Don Juan in Hell episode from *Man and Superman* and *The Man of Destiny* (1907), *The Dark Lady of the Sonnets* (1910), *Fanny's First Play* (1911) as well as individual dresses for Lillah McCarthy in a number of Shaw's plays, such as *Arms and the Man* (1907) and *Annajanska* (1918). Therefore Ricketts and Casson were at least on familiar terms, and Ricketts and Shaw were well used to one another's work. In this production Shaw was assisted as director by Casson, who also played de Stogumber, and Ricketts was assisted by Bruce Winston, who played de la Trémouille. The production generally was a happy combination of talented and creative persons, and it came at a critical point in several of their careers.

Ricketts had resigned himself to the lack of recognition for his stage designs. The new play was to establish his reputation firmly. Sybil Thorndike, who played Joan, needed a part of this caliber to show that she was more than a competent actress of wide-ranging abilities. Had the part come much later she would have been too old to portray convincingly the gauche inexperience of the Maid. Of course, once she established the part, the public was happy to go on seeing her play it for many years. For Shaw it was also a turning point in relation to his standing with the public. Certainly he always pretended to despise public opinion, but few men had greater need for an interested audience than Shaw.

The play's obvious humanity went a considerable way towards reinstating Shaw as the national mischief-maker, a teasing but eminently forgiveable prankster, after a long period of critical dismay over his major new works *Heartbreak House* (1917) and *Back to Methuselah* (1921), and public hostility over his statements about the recent war.[3] Though the epilogue to *Saint Joan* deliberately created mixed reactions in audiences who saw it, few could have left the theatre in any doubt that the aging, perhaps long-winded, dramatist's heart was, after all, in the right place. A letter to Lawrence Langner discussing the New York Theatre Guild's production a year earlier, in 1923, confirms the play's relevance to Shaw' vision of

> a world situation in which we see whole peoples perishing and dragging us towards the abyss which has swallowed them, all for want of any grasp of the political forces that move civilization.[4]

In this statement in a private letter Shaw spells out what he would never state straightforwardly in his plays. But any audience at a presentation of *Saint Joan* would realize that, despite the epilogue's implication that we lesser mortals will never change, the whole play is in fact a celebration of the triumph of the human spirit over political intrigue. Certainly this is how the play was received. In the popular esteem Shaw was once again the benign old jester.

The production was also an important breakthrough in the commercial London theatre scene. Many of Shaw's comedies such as *Candida* and *Fanny's First Play* had enjoyed long and successful runs. *Saint Joan*, though it is full of comedy, is not molded in the comic form and it was the first of his serious plays to be a great popular success. Its importance, therefore, goes beyond its effect on the individual careers of those involved and marks a major event in English theatre history. One thinks of Sir William Poel's summary of English theatre published just four years before *Saint Joan* was produced in London:

> The condition of the English Theatre has moved steadily downwards, and today it may be said to have touched its lowest level on record. The reason is not far to seek. The public has for so long seen theatrical amusements carried on as an industry, instead of as an art, that ...the plays of Shaw, Galsworthy, Barker, Masefield, with those of all men who respect themselves and their calling, are put on one side as being impossible compositions written by those who do not understand the needs of the public—meaning those who are not the Stock Exchange financiers.... The play-producing centre for the British Empire is London, and the men who control the output walk the pavements of Threadneedle Street.[5]

After *Saint Joan*, however, serious or artistic drama was more likely to be considered as financially viable. It is heartening to record that in this instance at least two of the beneficiaries of the production's success, Lewis Casson and Sybil Thorndike, put their monetary returns into further artistic endeavors, such as the revivals of *Henry VIII* (1925) and *Macbeth* (1926), for both of which Ricketts was again engaged as designer.

Saint Joan is a chronicle play. That is its essential design criterion. Shaw's full title is *Saint Joan: A Chronicle Play in Six Scenes and an Epilogue*, and it is always wise to pay attention to such formal definitions in Shaw's titles. The chronicle play as a literary form has never been bogged down with critical philosophy to the extent that tragedy and comedy have been. It has always been an essentially popular form of entertainment, a theatrical cartoon strip unfolding the lives, exploits and deaths of great men and women in a series of scenes which help to reveal their heroic characters. Margery M. Morgan has noted that, with its episodic series of trials and examinations of the heroine, *Saint Joan* bears some similarity to a medieval passion play.[6] The chronicle play as a dramatic form was very popular in the Elizabethan theatre, in such pageant dramas as Christopher Marlowe's *Tamburlaine the Great*, I and II. Since then this form had been largely overlooked until John Drinkwater revived it with considerable success in such plays as *Abraham Lincoln* (1918) and *Oliver Cromwell* (1921).

Chronicle plays with their episodic structure obviously create very specific design problems, quite different, for example, from a one-set tragedy like *Hedda Gabler*. Comparatively simple stage elements have to be employed to ensure quick transitions from one critical episode in the protagonist's life to the next. Yet, since the form has its roots in the medieval pageant-wagons of the passion plays, an element of exotic and historical spectacle is also appropriate. This combination of splendid historical effect and quick progression from scene to scene is difficult to achieve in any production, but in *Saint Joan* it is essential. Sybil Thorndike was fond of saying that Joan must "go down her road like a thunderbolt."[7] Yet the spectacle must also be provided to give the full flavor of medievalism and of a court—vain, self-indulgent and indolent at the expense of the people. The program for the original London production at the New Theatre makes it perfectly clear that in this three-and-a-half hour presentation there is no time for elaborate stage carpentry between scenes:

> The Curtain will be lowered between Scenes, but there will be only one interval after Scene Five,

and, after scene v:

> Interval of Ten Minutes.[8]

Some notion of the speed with which scenes were changed can be gauged from Jack Hawkins' memoir of a juvenile mishap. He played Dunois' page:

> There is a scene where Dunois and the Maid meet, and I was perched on a hillock guarding Dunois' great shield and lance. At the end of the scene, when Dunois and Joan are leaving the stage, I had to tug the lance from the ground, pick up the shield, and jump down to the rostrum, and from there down three steps to stage level, shouting: "The Maid, the Maid! God, and the Maid! Hurray-ay-ay!"
> Then according to the stage directions, I was to *caper out after them, mad with excitement.* I followed these directions faultlessly at the dress-rehearsal but by the time I hit the stage level

I had lost control of the heavy lance. The point swung forward and plunged through the extremely beautiful stage-drop which was then coming down.[9]

This stage drop was the blue, green and gold tapestry, *Saint Joan and Her Voices* (fig. 30), the design for which is now in the Bottomley Collection at Carlisle. From the quotation it would seem that the curtain was already on its way down before the actors were off the stage. Both the act drop and the various scenes which it reveals in quick succession must have gone some considerable way to creating the stylized medieval atmosphere Shaw desired without the inconvenience of:

two hours in building elaborate scenery, having real water in the River Loire and a real bridge across it, and staging an obviously sham fight for possession of it, with the victorious French led by Joan on a real horse.[10]

Since the improvisations of Bertolt Brecht (1898-1956) we have become used to the representation of chronicle plays in a different and equally valid style of production, but studying Ricketts' designs for *Saint Joan* one cannot but regret the recent total disappearance of act drops and all the old paraphernalia of scenic disclosure. In a recent article in *Plays and Players*, Gordon Gow also indulges his "nostalgia for the vanishing proscenium." He finds that the curtain has been replaced by something

in the manner of a cinema fade-in...hardly ever...sharpening the edge of expectation; or indeed commanding the attention to the same degree as a set freshly disclosed by a rising curtain,

or, one might add, contributing anything to the dramatic momentum of a pageant play or chronicle.[11]

Ricketts' designs for *Saint Joan* were an effective solution to the problem of creating a rich atmosphere of the medieval period by means of a series of easily changed stage pictures. Several of the original designs exist in various museums and Constable reproduced a considerable body of them in the limited edition of *Saint Joan* which they brought out to coincide with the first London production.[12] The production received a fair amount of publicity so there are also many production photographs showing the finished sets and costumes.

Scene i shows a sunny stone chamber on the first floor of a castle near Joan's family farm. All of the interior sets for this production remind us of Ricketts' statement that one can suggest more by a single staircase than by the painstaking recreation of a whole palace.[13] This setting shows the corner of a room, the principal feature of which is a high arched doorway leading off a turret staircase. Ricketts based this setting on the kitchen at Chilham Castle near Canterbury which his friends and patrons, Edmund and Mary Davis, had

Figure 30. *Saint Joan: Act Drop*
(Courtesy Bottomley Bequest, Carlisle)

recently acquired.[14] No actress could ask for a better entrance than Shaw has
built up for Joan in the dialogue between Robert de Baudricourt and the
steward. The narrow arched doorway Ricketts designed makes the entrance all
the more pleasing. A simple comparison between the photographs of the
London and New York productions shows Ricketts' superior sense of
theatre.[15] The squat archway in the New York production seems to press down
upon the figure of the actress, so that she has to fight against the proportions of
the set as well as the opposition of de Baudricourt. The upward thrust of
Ricketts' elegant entrance seems to precipitate the Maid's glorious career from
the very moments she steps on stage. The doorway also reminds one slightly of
the niche of some sculptured saint in a Gothic cathedral, so that from her very
first appearance Joan seems set off, framed in glory, a kind of icon. It is
interesting to note that what is no more than a subtle suggestion here of one
aspect of Joan's complex character was labored to the point of boredom in the
Pitoëff production of Shaw's *Saint Joan* in Paris (1925), in which the entire set
consisted of the three Gothic frames of a triptych in front of dark curtains, so
that all of the action took place in saintly surroundings, including the many
godless, mundane and even farcical moments of the play.[16]

The set for scene ii is divided by a great tapestry curtain which is later
drawn back to reveal the end of a throne room at Chinon. Figure 31 shows the
set with the tapestry closed, figure 32 the tapestry design itself. A study of the
production photographs shows that the stage was permanently fixed with a
flight of four steps and a raised level running right across the stage. The tapestry
curtain in this scene falls to the edge of the top step. It is split in the middle to
create an entrance and to allow for its being pulled back to either side of the
stage. The action of the earlier part of the scene takes place on the four steps. By
this device the set for scene i can be removed and the additional riser, thrones
and draperies, which define the full depth of the throne room in the later part of
the scene, can be brought into position.

The tapestry is the main feature of the setting. The design for this is in the
Fitzwilliam Museum, Cambridge (fig. 32), the design for the act drop tapestry
is in Carlisle, and the scale drawings or cartoons for both are in the Victoria and
Albert Museum, London. The pen, ink and wash cartoons are squared off to
show the scene-painters the scale of the figures. They also indicate colors with
touches of paint, and include instructions on how to achieve the textured effect
of ancient tapestry by means of repeated short vertical strokes of the brush,
using lighter tones against darker patches of color. This gives the appearance of
slightly uneven needlework catching the light from place to place. The effect
can be seen clearly in the rendering of grass and water in the red and green scene
ii tapestry (fig. 32). The coloring and style of the two designs derive from the
many fine examples of such works in the Musée de Cluny in Paris.[17] Perhaps
the blue, green and gold act drop (fig. 30) also owes something, particularly in
the stance of the figures, to the many pre-Raphaelite studies of medieval
knights and maidens.

Figure 31. *Saint Joan*: Scene II (before the tapestry) *(Courtesy Enthoven Collection, Victoria and Albert Museum)*

Figure 32.   *Saint Joan:* Tapestry Curtain, Scene II
(Courtesy *Fitzwilliam Museum, Cambridge*)

Appropriately enough the scene ii tapestry—which is the main visual clue to the court of France before Joan's entrance and rise to the leadership of the army—depicts knights and damsels sporting themselves in the Garden of Dalliance, while beyond the enclosure wall, death and battle ensue. The death scene depicts Pyramus and Thisbe; the battle scene shows *Mort* and *Amor*. The whole tapestry is a fine conceptualization of complex Shavian humor. It gives a clear indication of the understanding which existed between Shaw and Ricketts.

The act drop (fig. 30) shows Joan in an orchard, careless of her sheep, listening to the prompting of the saints while a figure representing France lies sleeping. It is interesting to note that Ricketts has canonized Joan even at this stage in her story, since she is shown with the saintly halo.

Figure 31 gives an idea of the scale of the curtain when one considers the size of the actors standing in front of it. One can imagine the colorful effect of the rich scarlet, black and metallic costumes against the subdued, antique coloring of the seemingly faded red and green tapestry, the contrast of the rounded, live characters against the stiff angular figures painted on the background.

When the tapestry is drawn back in scene ii it reveals two thrones on a dais. Immediately behind the thrones is a hanging panel depicting two angels with flags bearing royal insignia. The rest of the chamber is draped with curtains covered in the fleur-de-lis emblem of France. In the far background one can see the top of a high narrow stained-glass window. The acting area on top of the four steps which cross the whole width of the stage seems crowded, but some depth of field is achieved by positioning the two ushers in their bright costumes on the lower level at either side of the stage. The angle of their halberds helps to lead the eye up into the center of the action. The relatively small acting area exaggerates the cumbersome arrogance of the courtiers' costumes in contrast with Joan's workmanlike armor, a visual statement of the old town mouse-country mouse parallel.

At the conclusion of scene ii the act drop is lowered and a painted backdrop is brought into position about a third of the way back on the upper level. The act drop only need remain down long enough for the thrones to be replaced by a unit representing the clump of rock and grass, in which Dunois' pennon can be secured and against which his shield can rest.

In scene iii the permanent flight of four steps looks incongruous (fig. 33). What is a formal flight of steps doing beside the bank of a river? It is unfortunate that only production photographs of this scene exist and not the original design. Ricketts' easel paintings often showed figures in a landscape and there can be little doubt that he supervised the scene-painters competently in creating this backdrop. But it is an unfortunate scene for any designer because, to remain true to the text, the only way to create the scene quickly is with a flat, painted back cloth depicting the river. Yet this old-fashioned

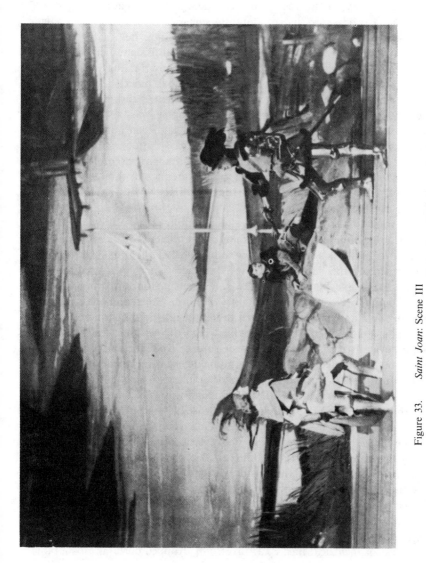

Figure 33. *Saint Joan:* Scene III
(*Courtesy Enthoven Collection, Victoria and Albert
Museum*)

method of stage decoration is out of keeping with most of the other scenes, which use one or two representative elements, such as an arch, a single pillar, a stained-glass window, two thrones on a rostrum, and great expanses of decorative drapery, to indicate some part of a larger space. The photographs of the New York production suggest that this scene was performed without a back cloth, relying simply on lighting to isolate the lance and pennon blowing in the wind. The New York designer obviously decided that this one element, the flag in the wind, is what the scene is about, and that the embarrassing business of the silver Loire in the background could be eliminated. Indeed the whole New York production seemed to rely heavily upon silhouette lighting at the expense of scenery. Of course, this designer, Raymond Dovery, was thousands of miles from Shaw and had a certain freedom which Ricketts had not. It is unlikely, however, that Ricketts would have used Dovery's solution as the whole text becomes ludicrous if the scene is performed other than in the semblance of clear daylight when kingfishers, boats and rippling water can be thought to be seen as well as the direction of the wind blowing on a flag. No other solution to the design of this scene suggests itself.

The transition from scene iii to scene iv requires the act drop for only as long as it takes to fetch on a table, chair and stool and to lower the curtains representing Warwick's tent into place in front of the flight of steps. The low unit representing the bank of the river and the painted backdrop could be removed during the playing of scene iv. A masking curtain would also be needed behind the center opening into the tent. Great diagonal bands of alternating light and dark colors, superimposed with various heraldic emblems and shields, are painted on the curtain which defines the tent. Warwick's heraldic device is repeated on the cover spread over the table. In the sepia design from the limited edition this heraldic device is repeated on Warwick's pennon which rests against his suit of armor, standing to one side of the stage. It is not clear whether or not this armor was actually used as it does not appear in any of the production photographs. In any case the multiplicity of symbols of heraldry on the walls of the tent make a visual statement about the political eminence of the occupier, Warwick. This aspect of power is increased by the fact that the emblazoned curtains fall in front of the steps , so that to enter the tent one has to descend from the outside world. Whether or not scene iii worked as a setting in its own terms, the contrast of the two consecutive scenes makes scene iv all the more effective. Scene iii with its natural setting, its humanity, its final manifestation of the efficacy of faith contrasts sharply with scene iv with its stylized nature in heraldic emblems, its urbanity, its edge of cynicism. From the simplest of theatrical means, a traverse or dropped curtain, plus a table, chair and stool, Ricketts creates a highly successful setting, full of medievalism, of pomp and circumstance and of political maneuvering. The use of heavy diagonal stripes helps to "cheat" the claustrophobic, tentlike effect in the shallow area that remains of the stage in front of the flight of steps. Some slight depth would be achieved when the entrance to the tent is held back.

Scene v represents the ambulatory of Reims Cathedral. This whole scene could be set while scene iv has been playing, some of it even during scene iii, as it is positioned fairly far back on the upper level. As the act drop rises Joan is revealed kneeling before the main element of the set, a massive round pillar to which is attached one of the stations of the cross. On one side of the pillar there is a screen of draped fabric and wood, rather like an organ screen, which forms an entrance to the vestry in the gap left between itself and the central pillar. One senses that beyond the pillar lies a great cloister receding into the far distance. This impression of depth is achieved by indications of a series of further pillars and screens going back into the distance till finally one-half of a high stained-glass rose window glimmers in the dark recesses of the cathedral. In this setting the upper level is used to great advantage. The feeling of depth would be less convincing if the dimly receding colonnade rose from the stage floor. By starting on the upper level it already seems far off. This effect can be seen in several of the production photographs. The shaft of light falling across the foot of the pillar, as if from a high window, also helps to create the illusion of distance beyond the pillar.

When the bright, pastoral act drop descends at the end of this scene it reminds us that Joan is indeed a saint, despite the gathering forces of darkness and her increasing isolation from former friends. At this point the program specifies an interval, which allows ten minutes to set the stage for the trial scene.

There is remarkable similarity in the staging of scenes ii and vi. Both use a further riser to elevate the two chairs of state, and both have a background of traverse curtains before another rank of higher curtains set further in the background, with stained-glass windows placed at the very back of the stage. In scene vi the stained-glass is obviously the same window of which we saw only a half section in scene v. Behind the raised chairs there hangs an immense crucifixion which reminds us that this is a bishop's court and not a court of law. The action spills over the steps at either end of the stage, with the executioner and his assistants on one side and the table for the scribes on the other. The principal visual effect of the scene is bound to be achieved by colorful assembly of the various ecclesiastics in their diverse robes bearing down upon the prisoner in her simple black page's uniform. Considering the rich hues of the religious habits, Ricketts seems to have left the background simple and muted. The most difficult aspect of the scene for a designer is the need to create an impression of some brightly lit courtyard, beyond the immediate setting of the trial, in which *"the glow and flicker of fire"* will eventually be seen *"reddening the May daylight."* One can only assume that Ricketts intended this effect to be suggested somewhere at the back of the stage beyond several ranges of curtains.

The act drop between scene vi and the epilogue conceals the biggest scene change of all. It is sound Shavian stagecraft which ensures that by the end of scene vi the stage is devoid of all but two actors and that the epilogue starts with only one, the dauphin, now Charles the Victorious, in his bed. Figure 34 shows the setting of this scene, which is not unlike the throne room in scene ii. Probably the crucifixion, the panel on which it hangs, the two chairs and their riser in scene vi were all of one piece and could simply be rolled off one end of the stage while the canopied bed was rolled on at the other. The dark draperies of the trial scene have been replaced by curtains of yellow and red with patterns of fleurs-de-lis alternating with sections of curving, wavering lines which would give Shaw's *"somewhat flamelike [effect] when the folds breathe in the wind."* Behind the curtains is a high lancet stained-glass window, probably the same as used in scene ii. There are a sufficient number of breaks and seams in the draperies to enable the ghostly visitors to slide into and out of the scene convincingly.

Beside Charles's bed there is a large arched painting of the Virgin and Holy Child (fig. 35). This prop is a typical example of the care Ricketts took with the smaller details of his designs. It is obviously the result of an intelligent response to the text. It is painted in the high courtly style of mid-fifteenth century French painting.[18] Surely there has never been a more worldly-wise Christ child with his coral toy, a more precious and enameled Virgin with her ermine robes, alabaster skin and painted cheek. Here is all the brittle sophistication of Charles' court, the flower of that French way of life Joan fought for, summed up in this travesty of devotional iconography. The Madonna is consistent with the whole setting and tone of this last scene, with its tongue-in-cheek dramatic effect and the clever manipulation of audience expectations with which Shaw denies us the emotional comforts of tragedy. In the closing moments of the play, Joan at her most devout speaks also for Shaw at his most ironic:

O God that madest this beautiful earth, when will it be ready to receive Thy saints? How long, O Lord, how long? [p. 208]

The irony of Ricketts' all too secular Madonna and Child neatly echoes Shaw's tone.

The principal costume designs have been reproduced in the limited edition of the play. They display Ricketts' creative powers when he was not restricted by strict interests of economy. As with the set designs Ricketts evokes a sense of specific period rather than a meticulous historical accuracy. The illuminated religious manuscripts of France, such as *Les Très Riches Heures du Duc de Berry*, are clearly his inspiration.[19] Ricketts uses these historical records merely as a springboard and therefore avoids the sickly sweetness of others who have depended upon such source materials—one thinks of the unbearably pretty French court scenes in Lawrence Olivier's film *Henry V*.[20] Ricketts adopts the bright luminous colors, the decorative details, the general line, but he makes the designs his own by the way he groups colors, by the exaggeration of motif

Figure 34. *Saint Joan*: King's Bedroom
(*Courtesy Enthoven Collection, Victoria and Albert Museum*)

Figure 35.   *Saint Joan*: Madonna (King's Bedroom)

and trimming. The general feeling of period, of an identifiably self-enclosed society is achieved by strict control of certain elements, such as complete concealment of hair—Joan being exceptional in this respect. Great emphasis, as usual, is laid on personal props, lances, pennants, jewels, purses, gloves and symbols of office and ritual.

The Constable of France, de la Trémouille, "a monstrous arrogant wineskin of a man" as Shaw describes him, was played by Bruce Winston, who assisted Ricketts with the costume (fig. 36).[21] Ricketts has designed a heavy black tunic which completely conceals the whole figure. It appears to be velvet decorated with a large gold repeated pattern. The costume has enormous open sleeves and a very high stiff collar. Both sleeves and hem are trimmed with fur. The tunic is closed by a narrow belt of white and purple wound several times around what should be the waist. Into this belt he has fastened one large white glove and a long, delicate rosary which is surely more decorative than spiritual in de la Trémouille's case. The pride of the figure culminates in a magnificent turban swathed in blue velvet. One great sweep of fabric is puffed up on the crown of the hat and two loose sections fall over the shoulders. Besides rings on both hands, he wears one large jewel on the front of the headdress and another heavy jewel, probably a chain of office, around his neck. As if this heavy costume was not enough to maneuver he wears a pair of ridiculously long, pointed shoes. Though supplied with a tapered stick, he holds this in such a dainty fashion with the little finger extended, that it cannot possibly be of use in supporting his enormous bulk.

His wife, La Duchesse de la Trémouille, wears a costume which is even more princely and unmanageable than his. It is very suitable for one who thinks of herself as queen of France and even masquerades as such when Joan is put to the test of identifying the dauphin in scene ii. The dress has a very low, square-cut neck, tight emerald sleeves decorated with gold buttons and ermine on the skirt, oversleeves and bodice. Black velvet side panels on the bodice prevent the costume from looking bulky. The deep hem and train are gold and black brocade. Head and ears are covered in a tight gold cap surmounted by a sweeping headdress trimmed with ermine and finished with a short white veil. She wears a choker necklace, a long pendant jewel and at least one large ring. The costume is a superb example of conspicuous display. One is hardly surprised that France cannot support a defensive war when the constable's wife dresses with such sumptuous excess.

Costumes of the other courtiers show a similar magnificent disregard for expense. One such design shows two courtiers, one male and one female. The lady wears a long-trained garment of gold and black brocade lined in crimson. This red is repeated as an insert at the neck and in a decorative detail where the dress is slit to the knee. She reveals one white silk stocking and a gold bracelet worn above the ankle. Both the hem and the bell-shaped sleeves are edged in brown fur. The headdress is a black cap topped with a gold bicorn trimmed

Figure 36.   *Saint Joan*: de la Trémouille

with ermine. Her lord wears a velvet mantle with the same flowing lines and cumbersome fur-trimmed sleeves and train. He wears a bright orange order of chivalry across his chest. Around his neck and shoulders there sits a high ermine collar and a yoke with a crenulated edge which is typical of several of the male costumes. Some contrast is provided by the crimson of his headdress and gloves. He wears white silk stockings and long, pointed shoes in black, white and red.

Another design reproduced in the limited edition shows a second courtly couple dressed in green and white with touches of black. The male figure wears a calf-length tunic decorated with heraldic lions. It has a deep hem checkered with patches of black and white fur. He wears the usual collar and yoke with crenulated edge. The full sleeves are lined with orange material and weighted with tassels. He wears a bracelet around the ankle and two separate gold chains around his shoulders. The headdress is a high square-blocked beaver with a feather decoration. His female companion wears a flowing overdress of green and white brocade, pointed black slippers and the familiar gold and ermine bicorn headdress over a tight black cap. Her oversleeves have scalloped edges and are decorated with gold braid and ermine tips. She wears gold fingerless gauntlets. Both figures play with spherical red toys.

A third design gives a front view of two ladies of the court, showing the two different lines used in the women's costumes. Both dresses have very low necklines and are caught up just under the bust. The black and gold dress hangs in ample folds from the artificially high waist. It has very full scalloped sleeves and a deep hem lined with scarlet. The blue and white dress has a quite different outline because the overdress has a waist slung low onto the hip. This overdress consists of layers of ermine alternating with blue and white brocade. It is worn over a black dress with light blue sleeves and has a vestigial oversleeve hanging from just above the elbow. One lady wears a bicorn headdress; the other has a large, highly decorated, gold hat. Both dresses have long sweeping trains. These costumes epitomize the useless arrogance of the court at a time of national crisis. Ricketts' designs remind us that one of Shaw's themes in *Saint Joan* is that natural patriotism springs from the people and not from political leaders whose first concerns are personal interests. These courtiers with their cumbersome folds, long trains, pointed shoes and top-heavy headdresses certainly would not be able to achieve much in a state of siege, but they might impress their peers in the invading army with the extent of their wealth and elegance.

The servants of the court are scarcely less elaborate than their superiors. The costumes of the two gentlemen ushers of the court are identical. Over tight green sleeves and red tights they wear loose white taberds lined in red. Each tunic is divided in the manner of a heraldic shield, half decorated with gold crowns, the other half with white on blue fleurs-de-lis. The calf-length hems and huge oversleeves have deeply slashed edges. The high yoke and collar exaggerate the shoulders so that the costume outline has very little relationship to the shape of the human body. Each usher wears a large green purse suspended from a loose waist-belt. The staff of office is more decorative than functional, striped in bands of blue and white with gold at both ends and topped with a gold fleur-de-lis.

Inevitably Charles, the dauphin, wears the drabbest costume of all the court. He is dressed fashionably but simply in black and grey. As Shaw indicates:

> he is a poor creature physically; and the current fashion of shaving closely, and hiding every scrap of hair... makes the worst of his appearance. [p. 99]

Over black stockings and pointed slippers he wears a black calf-length tunic of which the high collar, shoulder cape and hem are all trimmed with dark grey fur. His charcoal grey sleeves are caught into large gauntlets. The costume is bound with a white and gold belt and sword-carriage, which also supports a large black purse with gold tassels. The weakly figure is made to seem all the more helpless because of the huge beaver hat he wears pulled far down on his head, almost as if a child had tried on a top hat too large for him. The hat is decorated with a large jewel in front. Charles also wears a chain of office around his neck. It would have been easy to make this character ridiculous, but both Shaw in his stage directions and Ricketts in his design avoid this obvious course. Perhaps Ricketts remembered what a fine actor Ernest Thesiger had proved as Bagoas in Arnold Bennett's *Judith* despite the intentionally ridiculous concoction created for him as a costume for that part. In the *Saint Joan* design Thesiger has an almost spinsterish restraint compared with the lavish excess of the costumes for the other courtiers and the church dignitaries. The same design shows the Archbishop of Reims. He wears red hat, shoes and gloves together with a rich and ample robe of red and white. A deep ermine collar sits over the shoulders. Shaw dictates that there is *"nothing of the ecclesiastic about him except his imposing bearing"* (p. 97).

By comparison with the archbishop, Cauchon the Bishop of Beauvais must have presented a more dignified and austere appearance. His robe is not soft velvet and ermine but some harsh and shining material, possibly silk taffeta. It is cut full and wide with a flowing train and open sleeves. The top layer is mulberry colored, the inner sleeves and gauntlets are red. The design is notable for the black hood which visually associated Cauchon with the executioner, who wears a similar headgear. Indeed, Cauchon represents the ecclesiastical power which manipulates the course of Joan's fate. This visual linking of the bishop with the executioner is a telling example of Ricketts' concern for poetic rather than historical truth, as the black hood is not, and never was, appropriate to the dress of a bishop. Ricketts' intention as to the appearance of Cauchon is made clear by his drawing him in profile in such a way that the vulpine countenance contrasts ironically with the pastoral crosier he holds.

The design for the executioner shows him kneeling before Joan. He is simply dressed in black tights with a white shirt and black hood and gauntlets. Joan is shown in her magnificent armor from the coronation scene, worn with a blue and white tabard decorated with fleurs-de-lis. We know a certain amount about the armor, and the sword is now preserved in the Theatre Museum at Leighton House.[22] Shaw had definite opinions about the chain mail:

> It was by his direction that Sybil had real armour, which was extremely heavy to wear; he would not have any of the silver string concoctions that are so often used. He demanded "real chain armour which clatters as she walks." He and Ricketts had worked closely together on all the designs. . . . Ricketts had a definite influence on Shaw in the viusal aspects of the play, although he did not entirely agree with his concept of Joan. Ricketts would have preferred a more romantic figure.[23]

The design, in fact, shows not chain armor but beaten metal. Several of the production photographs show that the top half of the suit is chain mail, while the legs and arms are protected by metal pieces, as shown in the design. Joan, in fact, had a series of costumes; the simple red dress she wears in scene i, then the armor in scenes ii, iii, and iv with a relatively short workmanlike tabard, the armor again in scene v with the long blue and white tabard, as in the design. Ricketts takes poetic license when he shows her wearing this costume beside the executioner. Of course, during the trial scene she wears a simple black page's costume. Both this design and that of the book jacket for the limited edition show that Ricketts' concept was more romantic than Shaw intended. Both show a tall, boyish saint with very little of the flesh and blood farmer's daughter about her. The costume design depicts Joan with a transfixed, ecstatic look in her eye, as if already in love with the prospect of martyrdom. In the play Shaw demonstrates her natural love of life and reluctance to suffering. The book jacket design shows a resigned martyr rendered in a position which bears a deliberate similarity to the crucifixion of Christ. The production photographs show that Sybil Thorndike portrayed several facets of the Maid's character, some closer to Ricketts' concept, others closer to Shaw's. The romanticizing of the figure in the costume design obviously did not disturb Dame Sybil, as, until her recent death she kept the original of this design beside her in her sitting room.[24] Nor is there any evidence of a lasting difference of opinion between Ricketts and Shaw. Indeed Shaw was full of appreciation for the design:

> The Play has repeated its American success here: it is going like mad; and everybody, to my disgust, assures me that it is the best play I have ever written. Sybil Thorndike's acting and Charles Ricketts' stage pictures and costumes have carried everything before them.[25]

If *The Betrothal* designs had brought Ricketts to the attention of a discerning few his *Saint Joan* designs established him as the senior, practicing, British stage-designer of his day. Even critics such as A.B. Walkley of *The Times* noted that "the costumes designed by Mr. Charles Ricketts were a separate ecstacy."[26] For the few years remaining to him, Ricketts retained this leading position.

The working partnership of Sybil Thorndike, Lewis Casson and Charles Ricketts went on to create two further productions: *Henry VIII* at the Empire Theatre in 1925 and *Macbeth* at the Prince's Theatre in 1926. In both of these productions Ricketts developed ideas which he had used earlier. His inspiration for *Henry VIII* was the work of Holbein, the Tudor portrait-painter, from which he derived a muted palette of colors.[27] His stage pictures were, like those of *Saint Joan*, based upon the use of certain fixed points, such as pillars and risers; movable units, such as stained-glass windows; and highly decorated draperies and drops, used to cover or augment the fixed points as required. Again he used the idea of a curtain painted to represent the style and texture of a tapestry, but this time he took the concept one step further, in a most felicitous fashion. In the scene where Sybil Thorndike, playing the aging Queen Katherine, had her dream vision she was seated before a painted tapestry representing the heavenly host. The angels on the tapestry seemed to become substantial and surround the dreaming queen. The angels of the vision were child actors dressed exactly like the angels of the tapestry. The *Macbeth* designs continued with the same style of staging, though the stage's lack of depth created problems. Such designs and production photographs as exist show an imaginative use of ancient patterns and an assured handling of color. The production was not a success for a number of reasons—among other things Sybil Thorndike was unhappy with her costumes as Lady Macbeth. As a result, there was a cooling of the relationship between the Cassons and Ricketts.[28]

With *Saint Joan* Ricketts popularized the simplified historical method of presentation with which he had experimented as early as his *King Lear* at the Haymarket Theatre in 1909. It is always difficult to say who exactly originated a particular stage innovation. Suffice it to say that Ricketts' friends and contemporaries Norman Wilkinson and Albert Rutherston also pioneered this method of staging, but that *Saint Joan's* popularity created a recognizable school or style which can be seen in the work of a younger generation of designers: George Sheringham, Aubrey Hammond, Tanya Moiseiwitsch and Motley among others.[29]

7

Conclusion

I have examined five groups of plays in some detail. What emerges from this study is an overwhelming sense of artistic control. Ricketts himself has said wisely that there is no one style of stage decoration which will serve all types of drama.[1] Yet a study of his designs shows that, on the whole he chose to design plays which lent themselves to his specific abilities.

His costume designs demonstrate an assured sense of period conveyed by means of outline, gesture, fashion detail and hand properties—modified for the theatre by a masterly and highly personal handling of color, pattern and texture. Fine examples of this can be found in many of the designs I have discussed, but to give some sense of Ricketts' range I wish to refer to some of his other design projects and even to some which never reached the stage.

Throughout his life Ricketts amused himself by preparing designs for the operas of Wagner. Though they were sufficiently novel to rouse comment when exhibited, there was never much real possibility of these designs being carried through.[2] Fortunately many of the drawings have survived, though they are widely dispersed. One such design in the British Museum, a magnificent composition in its own right, shows Amfortas and two companion knights of the Holy Grail from *Parsifal*. Amfortas' great circular cape with its large-scale applied decoration might be from any number of Ricketts' productions, except for the details of the pattern which make it especially suitable for this opera.

As an artistic form opera appealed to Ricketts, just as it did to Shaw, because it presented the possibility of greater artistic control. Because it so often deals with quest for an ideal, leading to heroic resignation or death in the face of earthbound experience, opera also pleased Ricketts' sense of ritual action and artistic concentration. We find the recurring themes of his easel paintings, Don Juan, Montezuma, Judith, Salome repeated in his stage designs or projected designs for operas or plays in an elegiac mood which lend themselves to musical setting. As we have seen in *The Death of Tintagiles*, his designs are at their most imaginative when they relate to a combination of ritualized action, strange experience and heroic doom. Another fine example of this type of costume design can be seen in the superb series of designs for

Montezuma, a play which Ricketts persuaded his young friend Cecil Lewis to write. The play was never completed but many of the designs remain. Figure 37 shows how Ricketts adapted an entirely simple tunic into an impressive and exotic costume. Typical is his emphasis on headdress, sandals, jewelry and exaggerated pattern.

Ricketts' abilities were not confined to costumes for bizarre or idealized settings. As in his *Saint Joan* designs, Ricketts could, when appropriate, adapt historical sources to stage costumes with convincing and pleasing results. In this respect he was usually better informed than the general public, and sometimes the accurate knowledge of historical period which formed the background to his design work created hostility. Such was the case with *The Mikado* for which Ricketts designed new sets and costumes for Rupert D'Oyly Carte in 1926. Ricketts and Shannon had a considerable collection of Japanese works of art. There can be no doubt that Ricketts knew the exact historical background of this opera.[3] But the public has its own notions which no amount of scholarship can alter. In 1926 the received opinion of Japan was certainly not the same as Ricketts'. He was well aware of this, and had warned D'Oyly Carte of the public's preconceptions: "*The Geisha, Madama Butterfly*, and *The Mikado* have created a dreary pink dressing-gown style quite unlike anything Japanese."[4] Looking at the extant designs now it is hard to imagine such costumes causing adverse criticism. The designs show how Ricketts elaborated pattern on sleeves and hems in such a way as to force the company into an appropriate understanding of the grace and delicacy of Japanese gesture. This is an example of how Ricketts influenced the playing of roles by means of costume or property design. In this instance there is a happy ending. While his sets for *The Mikado* were replaced in 1962, the costumes created from his designs continued to be used till the company folded in 1982. There can be few examples of a designer's costumes still in use more than fifty years after their original creation. Few of the Gilbert and Sullivan devotees of this generation who have seen these costumes realize what a fuss they created in 1926.

In 1953 another set of costumes came to light unexpectedly, the original dresses which Ricketts had designed for John Masefields's *The Coming of Christ*. This nativity play was first presented in Canterbury Cathedral in 1928. Few of the original designs for this production exist, but thanks to Laurence Irving, who took part in both the 1928 production and the 1953 revival, the Enthoven Collection now has a number of photographs from the original production. Ricketts and Masefield took great care over the grouping of the players within the fine setting of the cathedral. Figure 38 also shows Ricketts' skill with softly draped fabrics as opposed to the stiffer, stenciled materials shown in some earlier photographs. In *The Coming of Christ* most of the applied pattern is restricted to wings, shields and pennants. Of the 1953 revival Alan Jefferson comments:

Figure 37.   *Montezuma*: Unidentified Figure
               (Courtesy Kirkaldy Museum and Art Gallery)

Figure 38. Masefield's *The Coming of Christ* (*Courtesy Enthoven Collection, Victoria and Albert Museum*)

Bishop Bell of Chichester ... had consented to lend Charles Ricketts' dresses from the 1928 production. These arrived from Canterbury and although they showed signs of storage and the passage of time ... they were in perfectly good order. We were astonished by their brilliance and vigour as they lay there unworn. ... Both houses on this December evening sat completely spellbound at Masefield's verse, at Gustave Holst's music, and especially at Charles Ricketts' costumes. ... The strongest contact with the earlier production was through the costumes that had spanned the gap of twenty-five years.[5]

For the Masefield play, the Christ child and most of the jewelry had been made by Ricketts himself. His letters of this period joke about this, his "third distinguished infant in the last two years, which is a kind of record for a bachelor."[6] One of these "distinguished infants" was the baby Elizabeth for the Cassons' production of *Henry VIII* in 1926. A letter to Gordon Bottomley (26 October 1926) gives some indication of Ricketts' attitude to prop making:

The baby Elizabeth, invisible from the front, has a cap and skirt with Tudor embroidery, silver swaddling clothes, gloves and jewels of pearl, coral and crystal made by me; the coral bough is of red wax. The fame of the doll spread through the company, and on the dress rehearsal, when the curtain was raised, all the Court ladies had instinctively crowded round the nurse to worship the infant as they might have done in real life.[7]

In costumes and settings he worked to compensate for the effects of distance in the theatre, but in props he was painstaking in his efforts to aid the actors' stage business and reactions.[8]

If Ricketts' set designs have now been largely forgotten it is perhaps because he was handicapped by the working conditions of the London theatres of his day, while his more famous contemporary Edward Gordon Craig produced designs which were, for the most part, created for ideal conditions and published to complement his theoretical studies. It is perhaps appropriate to quote here Ricketts' comments on a visit to Hart House Theatre at the University of Toronto. He visited Hart House in November 1927 while on tour in Canada as part of his duties in establishing the new National Gallery in Ottawa. He describes the theatre as a "good theatre with every appliance—they are giving *The Doctor's Dilemma* next."[9] Hart House is a comfortable college theatre but it has no fly space and very little wing space. That Ricketts found it a "good theatre with every appliance" gives some measure of the conditions in which he worked in some of the London theatres and halls of his day, though of course he also worked in such large, well-equipped houses as Covent Garden and the Coliseum. One is reminded of the difficulties Ricketts' had experienced just the year before his visit to Canada, in trying to fit his *Macbeth* designs onto the tiny proportions of the stage at the Prince's Theatre. He described this as being "like placing the Atlantic inside a duck-pond, or Durham Cathedral inside a bathing-machine."[10]

Ricketts' sets had a tendency towards literal representation which sometimes mixed incongruously with his otherwise commendable efforts to break up the flatness of the stage. We have noted an example of this in the Loire scene in *Saint Joan* where a painted backdrop of a river seems to rise out of a flight of steps. Yet a set-designer is limited by the demands of his text, as was certainly the case in this example. When freed from considerations of reality Ricketts' sets were imaginative, economical and telling. He could even combine painted backdrops with three-dimensional units effectively. One of his most attractive set designs is that for the throne room in the Palace of the Unborn Children which he designed in 1921 for Maeterlinck's *The Betrothal* (fig. 39). Here we see Ricketts' sense of formality, his use of semicircular staging, his happy mixture of minimal units (pillars, throne, dais, draperies) with a painted backdrop representing planets and cloud formations, his symbolic use of color to create poetic intensity.

Ricketts experimented with simplified or partial settings for scenes from historical plays to achieve quick transitions from scene to scene. His principle of "the part for the whole"—a flight of steps, a pillar, a stained-glass window instead of a complete palace or cathedral—occupied him till the last of his productions. This tendency surfaced brilliantly in his double scene from Ashley Dukes' adaptation of Frederick Bruckner's *Elizabeth of England*. This scene simultaneously shows Elizabeth in Westminster and Philip II in the Prado. Obviously Elizabeth's steps and throne and Philip's alter could be removed quickly to prepare for the next scene. This type of staging is now so common that we perhaps overlook Ricketts' innovation. In the final analysis it is the overall effect of costumes, props, lighting and sets which must be considered in any production. The Victoria and Albert Museum contains numerous rough costume sketches, prop designs, stage elevations and plans with indications as to light and shade for this, the last of Ricketts' design projects.[11] Studying this group of documents, one is impressed by the vigor and harmony of the designs. There is no sense of failing talents, of a designer overcome by personal trouble and working against time.

The last years of Ricketts' life were clouded by his companion's accident in 1929. From this time on Shannon needed constant nursing which was a strain on Ricketts' health, spirit and finances. During these years Ricketts began to sell parts of their celebrated art collection so that Shannon could receive adequate medical supervision. Shannon's physical health improved but he never regained his mental faculties. Ricketts died in his sleep on 7 October 1931, a week after the opening of *Elizabeth of England*. Shannon lived on till 18 March 1937.

An assessment of any artist's work inevitably includes a number of regrets and this must be the case with Ricketts. It is unfortunate that he came to stage design so late in his career, and that even then he continued to regard painting as his major work. That he was an accomplished painter naturally helped in the

Figure 39.   Maeterlinck's *The Betrothal*: Throne Room
(Courtesy Fitzwilliam Museum, Cambridge)

execution of his stage work. In choice of subject, his paintings were often representations of dramatic scenes. Yeats comments on this aspect of his work:

> Ricketts made pictures that suggest Delacroix by their colour and remind us by their theoretical composition that Talma once invoked the thunderbolt.[12]

Yeats' appraisal of Ricketts' paintings is not widely shared. Nevertheless it is unfortunate that an artist who could draw comparison with Talma's superhuman histrionics from the major dramatic poet of his day should have spent so much effort outside the theatre, in a medium which brought him little satisfaction. It is also to be regretted that when Ricketts did design for the stage he was very selective about the plays he would accept. For example, he only accepted *The Betrothal* out of loyalty to Granville Barker, yet, as a glance at figure 39 reveals, he produced at least one outstanding set design for this production. A stage-designer cannot afford to be too selective.

One must also regret that the designs of Ricketts and Craig were only seen together in Ireland. Who knows what might have resulted for the history of stage decoration in general, if these two designers could have produced in London those complementary designs seen together only in Dublin, through the efforts of Yeats. It is also unfortunate for Ricketts that Granville Barker decided to retire from the stage when he did. Granville Barker, Shaw, William Archer and others had planned a National Theatre at least as early as 1907.[13] Had these plans come to fruition, it seems likely that Granville Barker would have been the artistic director and that Ricketts would have been one of his senior designers. In this hypothetical case Ricketts would have been in an excellent position to influence designers of the younger generation to a far greater extent than he did. To some limited extent he did have an influence on younger designers, not least upon the simplified historical designs of the three young women who worked together under the name of Motley. In that Motley later taught for Michel Saint-Denis at the Old Vic Theatre School, one can trace a thin line of influence from Ricketts to the Old Vic, which for so long represented the closest thing Britain had to Granville Barker's idea of a National Theatre.

Most of all one must regret that the National Arts-Collection Fund, which acquired most of Ricketts' designs after his death, saw fit to split these up and distribute them, with no apparent logic as to selection, to so many isolated museums.[14] To take only one example, the designs for *Montezuma* known to be in public British collections are in the three major London museums and in Edinburgh, Hull, Kirkaldy, Leeds, Manchester and Portsmouth.

This means that I, who have visited most of these museums, have a greater familiarity with the whole range of Ricketts' designs than anyone else. It is an isolated position which I do not relish. In any case my knowledge must be imperfect. Even with photographs to aid one's memory, how much can one recall from so many museum visits in quick succession? The need for a major exhibition which pulls all the dispersed designs together into one place, at least for a short time, is manifest.

In my introduction I referred to Ricketts as representative of the classic pre-Raphaelite dilemma: on the one hand the tendency to recede into a perfect, artificial world surrounded by the arts of the past, on the other hand the urge to create a new order based upon what has been learned from the past. William Rothenstein also writes about Ricketts as depending "over much on conscious artistry," his "fatal desire" to influence others, his "*Einflusslust*," his "masterful personality which dominated all who came into contact with him."[15] Writing to Rothenstein, Sir Frederick Manning gives a more moderate view:

> Ricketts was much more of a magician than a philosopher. You spoke of his *Einflusslust*; that was the individual contingent, imp...selfconscious of the magician. I admire him because he did succeed in imposing it on his surrounding circumstances. He had so many technical accomplishments; but his real aim was to create for himself an illusion which would be more tolerable for him to live in than the real world, probably in dealing with the latter he had quite a practical appreciation of its necessities.[16]

Sir Charles Holmes finds that Ricketts' work for the stage acted as a kind of release from preoccupations with the aesthetic inheritance of the past:

> Ricketts' insight carried with it a subtlety in worldly affairs which was apt to be terrifying, until it was seen to be blended with the impulsive rapture of a child, not only in any beautiful thing, but in the music and pageantry of the theatre. To this, in his last years, Ricketts devoted much of his time, his inexhaustible fancy finding full play in the designing of scenery and costumes...his stage-settings, by common consent, were the most notable in modern times. Here, as in the books [which he designed], and in his astonishing brilliance as a talker (who else could fence so easily with Oscar Wilde?), his natural gifts had free expression: elsewhere his great acquired knowledge might seem at times to outweigh his instinct.[17]

On the stage Ricketts could create what Manning calls "an illusion which would be more tolerable for him to live in than the real world," a perfectly controlled world—be it some colorful period of the past, or some otherworldly symbolist ideal. By choosing only to work with those dramatists, directors and actors whose work he admired, he deliberately aligned himself with all the potential optimism, however naive, implicit in the serious and poetic drama of the first thirty years of this century.

Of course, in another sense, he influenced others in that his design work was a springboard for the younger generation of designers. Ricketts elevated the profession of stage design in Great Britain by bringing artist-designers into the theatre. He did this by working alongside his directors, not simply in a studio or in a scene-shop warehouse. He was in an excellent position to do this because he was a close friend of so many of the playwrights, directors and actors involved in the innovations in the new theatre of his day. Though many of the new plays were not financially successful they had considerable artistic impact, not least in the field of theatrical design. After Ricketts, close collaboration between director and designer became the established order in serious dramatic production. Towards the end of his life opening nights for productions which he had designed created as much anticipation as the appearance of some renowned star or the latest production by a famous director.[18]

A fitting appraisal with which to conclude is provided by T. Sturge Moore:

> Work for the stage was for Ricketts a holiday task. The dramatist had lifted from his shoulders the fundamental decisions which exhaust as they reveal [relieve?] the spirit. All was comparatively plain sailing. His sketches for costumes were often able to inspire an actress or elicit the mood of a part, and several of our best artists learnt to expect from him invaluable suggestions for business or gesture. . . . Some thought he wasted his time on details that could not tell, but he realized that they added a sense of more to see, which is like bloom on fruit to stage effect. He knew how to drive the accents of historical costume farther in the same direction, so as to make them effective at a distance. For colour, pattern, and cut his designs were pre-eminent. He did not attempt to revolutionize or to lay down new principles, being persuaded that the thirst for violent change was always due to inappreciative ignorance or pedantic fanaticism. He accepted the means that lay at hand; they had been ill-used or degraded, he felt he could ennoble them.[19]

Appendix A

Productions Designed by Ricketts

This listing excludes projected productions which did not reach the stage.

1906,	?	*Astarte*, by T. Sturge Moore. Literary Theatre Society.
	March 8	*Paris and Oenone*, by Laurence Binyon. Savoy Theatre.
	April 1	*Aphrodite against Artemis*, by T. Sturge Moore.
	June 10	*Salome*, by Oscar Wilde, and *A Florentine Tragedy*, by Oscar Wilde. Literary Theatre Society.
1907,	March 23	*A Miracle*, by H. Granville Barker, and *Persians*, by Aeschylus. Literary Theatre Society.
	June 4	*Don Juan in Hell*, and *The Man of Destiny*, both by Bernard Shaw. Court Theatre.
	Sept. 4	*Attila*, by Laurence Binyon. His Majesty's Theatre.
	Dec. 30	*Arms and the Man*, by Bernard Shaw. (Lillah McCarthy's costume only.) Savoy Theatre.
1908,	May 14	*Lanval*, by Lord Howard de Walden. Playhouse Theatre, transferred to Aldwych Theatre.
	Sept. 19	*A Florentine Tragedy*, by Oscar Wilde. Lyceum Theatre, Edinburgh.
	Sept. 27	*Electra*, by Arthur Symons from Hofmannsthal. New Theatre.
1909,	Sept. 8	*King Lear*. Haymarket Theatre.
1910,	Nov. 24	*The Dark Lady of the Sonnets*, by Bernard Shaw. Haymarket Theatre.
1911,	April 19	*Fanny's First Play*, by Bernard Shaw. Little Theatre.
	?	*King Lear*. For a Japanese company, New Theatre, Tokyo.
	?	*One Act Plays*, by Gordon Bottomley. (It seems likely that Ricketts designed some short plays of Bottomley's at about this time—from production photographs in the Witt Library.)

1912,	Jan.	*Oedipus Rex,* by Gilbert Murray from Euripides, for Max Reinhardt. (Lillah McCarthy's costume only.) Covent Garden.
	Dec. 17	*The Death of Tintagiles,* by Alfred Sutro from Maeterlinck. St. James's Theatre. Revived Savoy Theatre, 1913.
1914,	June 12	*The King's Threshold,* by W.B. Yeats. Court Theatre.
	Nov. 5	*Philip the King,* by John Masefield. Covent Garden.
	Nov. 25	*The Dynasts,* adapted from Thomas Hardy by H. Granville Barker. Kingsway Theatre.
1915,	Jan. 27	*The Man who Married a Dumb Wife,* by Anatole France. Wallach's Theatre, New York. Revived Ambassador's Theatre, London, 1917. (Ricketts designed some of the costumes.)
	May/June	*The Well of the Saints,* by J.M. Synge, and *On Baile's Strand,* by W.B. Yeats. Little Theatre.
1916	Jan.	*Judith,* by T. Sturge Moore. Queen's Theatre.
	May 19	*Lithuania,* by Rupert Brooke. His Majesty's Theatre.
	June	*A Door Must be Open or Shut,* by Alfred de Musset.
	June 9	*The Admirable Crichton,* by J.M. Barrie. (Lillah McCarthy's costume only.) Coliseum Theatre.
1918,	Jan. 21	*Annajanska,* by Bernard Shaw. Coliseum Theatre.
	Sept.	*Twelfth Night, The Merchant of Venice* and *Two Gentlemen of Verona.* Lena Ashwell company for army camps in France.
1919,	April 30	*Judith,* by Arnold Bennett. Kingsway Theatre, London. (Original opening in Eastbourne.)
	July 18	*Näil,* by Isidore de Lara. Covent Garden.
	?	*Salome,* by Oscar Wilde. Shōchiku Company, Tokyo.
1920,	?	*Alcestis, Medea,* and *Iphigenia in Tauris.* For Mrs. Penelope Wheeler's touring company.
1921,	Jan. 8	*The Betrothal,* by Maeterlinck. Gaiety Theatre.
1924,	March 26	*Saint Joan,* by Bernard Shaw. New Theatre.
1925,	Dec. 23	*Henry VIII.* Empire Theatre.
1926,	Sept. 20	*The Mikado,* by Gilbert & Sullivan. Savoy Theatre.
	Dec. 24	*Macbeth.* Prince's Theatre.

1928,   May 28   *The Coming of Christ,* by John Masefield. Canterbury Cathedral.

1929,   Oct. 21   *The Gondoliers,* by Gilbert & Sullivan. Savoy Theatre.

1931   June   *Sarah Siddons, the Greatest of the Kembles.* Kemble Theatre, Hereford.

         Sept. 30   *Elizabeth of England,* by Ashley Dukes from Frederick Bruckner. Cambridge Theatre.

Appendix B

A Finding List of Ricketts' Designs

This listing excludes photographs of designs and production photographs.

	Location
The Admirable Crichton	
Costume design: Lady Mary	Yale
Agamemnon	
Set design	V. & A.
Antigone	
Set design	V. & A.
The Betrothal	
Set design: Throne Room	Fitzwilliam
Backdrop design: [Throne Room]	Walker, Liverpool
The Bride of Dionysus	
Set design	Sunderland
The Coming of Christ	
Costume design: Roman Soldier	V. & A.
Costume design: Gaspar	Bell Estate
Costume design: Angel	Bell Estate
The Death of Tintagiles	
3 unspecified designs	Harvard
Costume design: Bellangère	Carlisle
Costume design: Ygraine and Tintagiles	Carlisle
Costume design: Anglovale	Carlisle
Costume design: Servant of the Queen	Carlisle
Costume design: Three Servants of the Queen	V. & A.
The Dynasts	
Costume design	Harvard
Elizabeth of England	
Set design	Manchester
Set design	Blackburn
Costume design: Elizabeth	V. & A.

The Eumenides
Set design   V. & A.

Faust
Set design: Faust's Study   V. & A.

A Florentine Tragedy
3 costume designs   U.C.L.A.

Henry VIII
Backdrop   V. & A.
Set design   V. & A.
Set design   Reading
Design for stained-glass backdrop   Bristol
Design for "tapestry:" Katharine's Vision   Swansea

Irish Plays
Costume design: Mayor of Kinvara   V. & A.
Molly Byrne   Anne Yeats
Molly Byrne in her Wedding Shawl   Anne Yeats
Deirdre and Lavarcham   Anne Yeats
Deirdre   Anne Yeats
Conchobor   Anne Yeats
King Guaire   Anne Yeats
Princess   Anne Yeats
"Angus" [Seanchan]   Anne Yeats
Blind Man   Anne Yeats
Fool   Anne Yeats
Blind Man and Fool   Anne Yeats
Three Singing Women   Anne Yeats
Four Kings   Anne Yeats
King   Anne Yeats
Old King   Anne Yeats
Cuchulain   Anne Yeats

Bennett's *Judith*
Costume design: Judith   Derby
Costume design: Judith   Fine Art Society
Costume design: Jewish Dancer   V. & A.
Costume design: Holofernes   Leeds
Costume design: Attendant on Holofernes   V. & A.
Costume design: [Unidentified Eastern Figure]   Ashmolean
Costume design: [Eastern Female and Child]   Sheffield
10 unspecified costume designs   Harvard
Costume design: [Eunuch]   Fine Art Society
3 unspecified costume designs: Women of the Tent   Fine Art Society
Costume design: [Judith's maid]   Ashmolean

Sturge Moore's *Judith*
Set design   Carl Woodring
Costume design: Judith   Carl Woodring

King Lear
Set design: Lear's Palace   V. & A.
Costume design: Goneral   V. & A.

Macbeth
Set design: Banquet Hall   Nottingham
Set design   V. & A.
Costume design: Lady Macbeth   Bradford

The Man who Married a Dumb Wife
Costume design: The Wife   V. & A.
5 costume designs   Harvard

The Mikado
Costume design: Katisha   V. & A.
Costume design: 2 Female Figures   Exeter
Costume design: 2 Ladies of the Chorus   Ulster
Costume design: Male Figure   Edinburgh
Costume design: Male Figure   Edinburgh
Costume design: 3 Figures   V. & A.

Modern Stage Setting
Design for book jacket   V. & A.

Montezuma
Set design: Throne Room   Manchester
Set design: Epilogue   V. & A.
Act drop curtain design   Leeds
Costume design: Devil   Edinburgh
Costume design   Hull
Costume design   Portsmouth
Costume design   V. & A.
Costume design: Warrior   Tate
Costume design: Master and Servant   Tate
Costume design: Dying Warrior   Manchester
2 costume designs: Unidentified Male Figures   B.M.
Costume design: Unidentified Male Figure   Manchester
Costume design: Unidentified Male Figure   Kirkaldy

Pagliacci
Set design   Newcastle

Parsifal
Set design   Bradford
Set design: Forest [probably *Parsival*]   Fitzwilliam
Set design: Act I, Scene 4   Nottingham
Set design   Bootle
Costume design: Amfortas and 2 Companion Knights   B.M.
Costume design: Amfortas   Charles Gullans
Costume design: Male Figure   B.M.

Rheingold
Set design   Manchester

Saint Joan
Act drop: Saint Joan and Her Voices   Carlisle
Design for "tapestry:" Scene II   Fitzwilliam
Set design: King's Bedroom   Walker, Liverpool
Panel from cathedral scene (painted by Ricketts)   Thorndike Estate
Costume design: Saint Joan and Executioner   Thorndike Estate
Costume design: 2 Ladies of the Court   V. & A.

Sakuntala
Costume design: Buffoon   V. & A.
Costume design: Prince   Ashmolean

Salome
Set design   V. & A.
Set design: Japanese Version   Fitzwilliam
Costume design: Soldiers and Slave   V. & A.
Costume design: Young Syrian   V. & A.
Costume design: Negro [Executioner]   Ashmolean
Costume sketch: Salome   V. & A.
Costume design: Romans   Lincoln
Costume design: Jewish Priests   V. & A.
Costume design: Herodias   V. & A.
Costume design: Herod   Tate

Shakespeare (Y.M.C.A.-War Front Concerts—Interchangeable costumes for the Italian
comedies)
Costume design: Female Figure   Ashmolean
Costume design: Doge of Venice   Bournmouth
Costume design: Jessica   Brighton
Costume design: Tubal   Tate
Costume design: Balthazar   Norwich

Shakespeare (settings which form illustrations to Ricketts' book *Shakespeare's Heroines*—original
designs are in the following locations)
Set design: *Othello*   V. & A.
Set design: *Twelfth Night*   V. & A.
Set design: *Romeo and Juliet:* Balcony   B.M.
Set design: *Romeo and Juliet:* Tomb   B.M.
Set design: *Merchant of Venice*   Whitworth

Mrs. Siddons Memorial Celebration
Costume design: Lillah McCarthy as Siddons   Harvard
in *Macbeth*

Siegfried
Costume design: Siegfried   Ashmolean

Tristan and Isolde
Set design   Hove
Set design: Act I   Carlisle
Costume design: Tristan   Carlisle

Twilight of the Gods
Set design   Sunderland

Winter's Tale
Set design: Trial scene   Bath
Set design: Unspecified   Newcastle
Set design: Finding of Perdita   Manchester
Costume designs: Leontes (two versions of same)   Hove
Costume design: Leontes (another version of above)   V. & A.
Costume design: Hermione   V. & A.
Costume design: [Florizal]   Fitzwilliam
Costume design: 2 Figures   B.M.
Costume design: 2 Figures   Manchester
Costume design: Female Figure   Kettering
Costume design: 2 Female Figures   Ipswich
Costume design: 2 Female Figures   Fitzwilliam
Costume design: 2 Courtiers   Cardiff

Witch Dance
Costume design: Oriental Kneeling Figure   Ashmolean

Unidentified
Set design   B.M.
Costume design   Stoke-on-Trent

Volume of working drawings and
rough sketches for several plays   V. & A. 92D33

Key to Locations

Ashmolean	Ashmolean Museum of Art & Archeology, Oxford
Bath	Holborne of Menstrie Museum, University of Bath
Blackburn	Blackburn Museum of Art Gallery
Bootle	Bootle Museum and Art Gallery
Bournemouth	Russell-Cotes Art Gallery & Museum, Bournemouth
Bradford	Bradford City Art Gallery and Museum
Brighton	Brighton Museum and Art Gallery
Bristol	Bristol City Art Gallery
B.M.	British Museum (Department of Prints & Drawings), London
Cardiff	National Museum of Wales, Cardiff
Carlisle	Bottomley Bequest, Carlisle Museum, Art Gallery and Public Library
Derby	Derby Museum and Art Gallery
Edinburgh	Scottish National Gallery of Modern Art, Edinburgh
Exeter	Royal Albert Memorial & Art Gallery, Exeter

Fine Art Society	Fine Art Society, New Bond Street, London
Fitzwilliam	Fitzwilliam Museum, Cambridge
Harvard	Harvard Theatre Collection, Harvard University
Hove	Hove Museum & Art Gallery
Hull	Ferens Art Gallery, Kingston upon Hull
Ipswich	Ipswich Museum and Art Gallery
Kettering	Alfred East Art Gallery, Kettering
Kirkaldy	Kirkaldy Museums and Art Gallery
Leeds	Leeds City Art Gallery
Lincoln	Usher Art Gallery, Lincoln
Manchester	City Art Gallery, Manchester
Newcastle	Laing Art Gallery & Museum, Newcastle-upon-Tyne
Norwich	Norwich Castle Museum, Norwich
Nottingham	Nottingham City Museum and Art Gallery
Portsmouth	Portsmouth Public Library and Museum
Reading	Reading Museum and Art Gallery
Sheffield	Mappin Art Gallery, Sheffield
Stoke	Stoke-on-Trent Museum and Art Gallery
Sunderland	Sunderland Central Museum & Art Gallery
Swansea	Glynn Vivian Art Gallery, Swansea
Tate	Tate Gallery, London
Ulster	Ulster Museum Art Gallery
U.C.L.A.	William Andrew Clark Memorial Library, University of California, Los Angeles
V. & A.	Victoria and Albert Museum, London
Walker, Liverpool	Walker Art Gallery, Liverpool
Whitworth	Whitworth Art Gallery, Manchester
Yale	Yale University Library, New Haven, Connecticut

"Bell Estate" and "Thorndike Estate" indicate the executors of the late Bishop Bell and Mrs. Bell of Chichester, and the executors of the late Dame Sybil Thorndike Casson, respectively. They, Charles Gullans (U.C.L.A.), Carl Woodring (Columbia University) and Miss Anne Yeats hold private collections of Ricketts' designs.

The Fine Art Society, New Bond Street, London is a commercial gallery. While this establishment has shown several of Ricketts' works from time to time, its aim is to sell such works.

Notes

Chapter 1

1. Kenneth Clark, *Another Part of the Wood* (London: John Murray, 1977), pp. 178-79.

2. George Bernard Shaw, *Collected Letters, 1874-1910,* edited by Dan H. Laurence. 2 vols. (London: Bodley Head, 1970), II, pp. 97-99.

3. Laurence Binyon (1869-1943), poet, dramatist, art historian, Keeper of Prints and Drawings at the British Museum. William Orchardson (1832-1910), genre painter, Scots expatriate in London. Bernard Berenson (1854-1957), art historian, authority on Italian painting. William Rothenstein (1872-1945), portrait-painter, lithographer and writer.

4. Charles Hazelwood Shannon (1863-1937), lithographer and portrait-painter, collector. He and Ricketts were lifelong friends and first set up house together in rooms adjoining the Vale, King's Road, Chelsea (formerly the home of Whistler) from which they ran the Vale Press. Later they moved to studios in Lansdowne House, Holland Park which had been altered by their patron Sir Edmund Davis, so that Ricketts and Shannon could live on the top of his house. In 1924 they moved to Townsend House at St. John's Wood. They also had a country retreat at the Keep, Chilham Castle in Kent, which was given to them for life by Sir Edmund and Lady Davis.

5. Charles Ricketts, *Self-Portrait: Letters and Journals of Charles Ricketts,* compiled by T. Sturge Moore, edited by Cecil Lewis (London: Peter Davis, 1939), p. 52.

6. Diaries, 13 August 1914. British Library MS. 58105.

7. Ricketts, *Self-Portrait,* p. 380, note.

8. Scheme for Slade Lectures. British Library MS. 58085.

9. Diaries, 2 March 1914. British Library MS. 58105, referring to a review of an exhibition of Ricketts' and Shannon's paintings in New York, in which the reviewer described them as "Post-Raphaelites."

10. The opinion of Sir Walter Raleigh, reported to Ricketts by Mrs. Laura Anning Bell, quoted in *Self-Portrait,* p. 268.

11. British Library MSS. 58105 and 58106. Despite the statement that he was glad not to have seen Reims before it was damaged, he resolved to set out immediately to visit the great English churches, Winchester, St. Cross, Romsey, Salisbury. The Baudry ceilings at the Opéra have since been painted over with designs by Chagall.

12. Ricketts, *Self-Portrait,* pp. 231-32.

13.   Ibid., p. 250.

14.   Ibid., p. 261.

15.   Ibid., p. 51. It was Ricketts' custom to make a summary of the year at the end of each volume of his diaries. This is taken from the summary for 1900—a year made especially painful for him by the death of his old friend Oscar Wilde.

16.   John Ruskin, *Selections and Essays*, edited by Frederick William Roe (New York: Scribner, 1918), p. 246.

17.   William Morris, *Selected Writings and Designs*, edited by Asa Briggs (Harmondsworth: Penguin, 1962), p. 68.

18.   Philippe Auguste Villiers de l'Isle Adam, *Axël*, trans. by June Guicharnaud (Englewood Cliffs: Prentice - Hall, 1970), pp. 182-83.

19.   Joris-Karl Huysmans, *A Rebours* (Paris: G. Cres, 1922), p. 29.

20.   Charles Ricketts, *Charles Ricketts R.A.: Sixty-Five Illustrations*, introduced by T. Sturge Moore (London: Cassell, 1932), [vii-viii]. Future references to this work are to *Sixty-Five Illustrations*.

21.   Jacques-Emile Blanche, *Portraits of a Lifetime, 1870-1914*, (London: Dent, 1933), pp. 130-31.

22.   Ricketts, *Self-Portrait*, p. 43.

23.   Diaries, British Library MS. 58106.

24.   Ricketts, *Sixty-Five Illustrations*, [xvi].

25.   Gordon Bottomley, *Poet & Painter: Correspondence between Gordon Bottomley and Paul Nash: 1910-1946*, edited by Claude Colleer Abbott and Anthony Bertram (London: Oxford University Press, 1955), p. 3.

26.   Ibid., p. 3, note.

27.   Ibid., p. 123.

28.   Ricketts, *Self-Portrait*, p. 54, note.

29.   William Rothenstein, *Since Fifty* (London: Faber, 1939), pp. 60-61.

30.   Thomas Lowinsky, in *The Dictionary of National Biography, Supplement 1931-1940*, edited by L.G. Wickham Legg (London: Oxford University Press, 1949), p. 732.

31.   See Sheldon Cheney, *Stage Decoration* (London: Chapman & Hall, 1923), for discussion of developments culminating in the work of Appia and Craig.

32.   Diaries, 27 December 1904. British Library MS. 58102.

33.   Republished, with slight changes, in Ricketts' collection of essays, *Pages on Art* (London: Constable, 1913), pp. 229-49.

34.   George Bernard Shaw, *Our Theatre in the Nineties*, 3 vols. (London: Constable, 1932), I, p. 165.

35.   Appendix V to Chapter IV of Ernest Reynolds, *Modern English Drama* (Norman, Oklahoma: University of Oklahoma Press, 1951), pp. 210-11.

36.   Charles Ricketts, "The Art of Stage Decoration," in *Pages on Art*, p. 236.

37.   Ibid., pp. 234-35.

38.   Ibid., p. 237.

39.   Ibid., 246, note.

40.   Ibid., p. 242.

41.   Ibid., pp. 230-31.

42.   Ibid., p. 240.

43.   Ibid., p. 246.

44.   Ibid., p. 229.

45.   Ibid., p. 248.

46.   Ibid., p. 249.

Chapter 2

1.   Kyrle Ifan Fletcher, "Charles Ricketts and the Theatre," *Theatre Notebook*, 22 (1967), p. 21.

2.   As many of the actors involved would have had other professional engagements, its central position close to Shaftsbury Avenue would also have recommended it.

3.   The various productions and projected productions discussed here may be listed: (1) Bernhardt in rehearsal, London, 1892, banned by the Lord Chamberlain; (2) Lugné-Poe production at the Théâtre de l'Oeuvre, 1896; (3) production at the Bijou Theatre, London, 1905; (4) Literary Theatre production, King's Hall, London, 1906, designed by Ricketts and (5) projected production, Shōchiku Company, Tokyo, 1919.

4.   About this time the name changed from "Literary Theatre Club" to "Literary Theatre Society."

5.   In 1895 Oscar Wilde had been sentenced to imprisonment for moral offences. As a result of his disgrace no commercial management in Britain dared to produce any of his plays. In any case, *Salome* had already been censored in 1892 because it would have represented Biblical characters on stage.

6.   Ricketts, *Pages on Art*, pp. 243-44.

7.   Ricketts, *Self-Portrait*, p. 137, note.

8.   Diaries, 22 March 1906, British Library MS. 58104. In fact the role of John the Baptist (or Jokanaan) was played by the young Lewis Casson with considerable success. This was the start of a long working association between Ricketts and Casson.

9.   Diaries, April and May 1906, British Library MS. 58104.

10.   Ibid., 3 April and 9 April 1906.

11.   Many of the professional actors drawn to the new literary theatre groups had been trained in this way in the old provincial touring companies.

12.   Ricketts, *Self-Portrait*, p. 136.

13.   A number of Ricketts' costume sketches for *A Florentine Tragedy* are in the Clark Memorial Library, U.C.L.A.

14. Adolphe Appia (1862-1928), influential Swiss scenic designer and theorist. Illustrations of his design projects are reproduced in several works, among them Denis Bablet's *Esthétique Général du Décor de Théâtre de 1870 à 1914* (Paris: Centre National de la Recherche Scientifique, 1965), figs. 85-112.

15. Ricketts, *Self-Portrait*, p. 137.

16. British Library MSS. 45851-56. This particular quotation is also reproduced in Michael Field, *Extracts from Work and Days: Extracts from the Journals of Michael Field*, edited by T. Sturge Moore and D.C. Sturge Moore (London: John Murray, 1933), pp. 249-50.

17. Many attempts have been made to define the celebrated Abbey style of acting. Willie Fay suggests that to some extent it derived from the inexperience of the company. See William G. Fay and Catherine Carswell, *The Fays of the Abbey Theatre* (London: Rich and Cowan, 1935), pp. 207-10. Yeats' aim was that the actors should seem to be "impassioned and yet to have a perfect self-possession, to have a precision so absolute that the slightest inflection of voice, the slightest rhythm of sound or emotion plucks the heart strings." *The Letters of W.B. Yeats*, edited by Allan Wade (New York: Macmillan, 1955), p. 360. Some combination of Fay's opinion and Yeats' theory created a memorable style from as early as 1903, the first Abbey tour. At times Florence Farr came close to Yeats' ideal, and the playwright had equal hopes for Letitia Darragh.

18. Max Beerbohm, *Last Theatres: 1904-1910* (London: Hart-Davis, 1970), pp. 249-52.

19. Gertrude R. Jasper, *Adventure in the Theatre: Lugné-Poe and the Théâtre de l'Oeuvre* (New Brunswick: Rutgers University Press, 1947), p. 208.

20. In 1901 Yeats had brought Letitia Darragh to Dublin to act with the Abbey company. She had some critical success but was unpopular with the other actors, who resented her presence.

21. Ricketts, *Self-Portrait*, p. 319.

22. Gordon Bottomley, "Charles Ricketts R.A.," *Theatre Arts Monthly*, 16 (1932), p. 381.

23. Page references are to Oscar Wilde, *Complete Works*, edited by Vyvyan Holland, 2nd rev. ed. (London: Collins, 1966).

24. Ricketts' own description of the earlier design, which had been subject to a strict budget (*Pages on Art*, p. 244).

25. Ibid., p. 244.

26. Robert Ross, *Friend of Friends*, edited by Margery Ross (London: Jonathan Cape, 1952).

27. Bottomley, "Charles Ricketts R.A.," pp. 380-81.

28. With the exception of the Victoria and Albert Museum, few collections have tried to identify designs. More often than not a design will be listed simply as, e.g., "unidentified male figure." I have given titles to the drawings which I discuss and noted any puzzling designs.

29. Ricketts painted several works on the theme of Don Juan, one of these may be seen in the Tate Gallery, London, Tate 3221.

30. Victoria and Albert Museum, London. A folio of rough sketches pasted into a scrapbook, with tentative attributions, possibly by T. Sturge Moore; V. & A., Prints and Drawings 92D33.

31. For example, Augustin Pitt-Rivers, *Antique Works of Art from Benin* (1900; reprint ed., New York: Hacker Art Books, 1968), p. 75, fig. 286.

32.   Ricketts, *Pages on Art*, p. 244.

33.   Ricketts, *Self-Portrait*, pp. 135-36.

34.   Ross, *Friend of Friends*, p. 127.

35.   Roger Fry, *Letters*, edited by Denys Sutton. 2 vols. (London: Chatto & Windus, 1972), I, p. 267.

Chapter 3

1.   André Gide, *Journals: 1899-1939* (Paris: Gallimard, 1948), p. 194.

2.   C.B. Purdom, *Harley Granville Barker: Man of the Theatre, Dramatist and Scholar* (London: Rockliff, 1955), p. 9.

3.   Fletcher, "Charles Ricketts and the Theatre," 15.

4.   Most of the critical studies of Maeterlinck mention this aspect of his changing views, e.g., Montrose J. Moses, *Maurice Maeterlinck: A Study* (New York, Duffield, 1911).

5.   Gide, *Journals: 1889-1939*, p. 194.

6.   References to the text are to Maurice Maeterlinck, *Three Plays*, introduced by Harley Granville Barker (London: Gowans & Gray, 1911). This would seem the text most likely to have been used by Ricketts.

7.   Bablet, *Décor de Théâtre*, p. 175. Meyerhold's interest in productions which had a two-dimensional resemblance to icons was short-lived. He is best remembered for his work using constructivist sets which were essentially three-dimensional in appearance.

8.   Oscar Fischel, *Das Modern Buhnenbild* (Berlin: Wasmith A.-G., [1923]), p. 48, wrongly identifies this design as "Figure zu den Tochtern des Konig Lear."

9.   Bottomley, "Charles Ricketts R.A.," pp. 377-[90].

10.   The role of the boy was played by a young girl, Odette Goimbault.

11.   Cecil Lewis has described Ricketts' working methods: "I have seen him create designs for a production in one day. They were dashed off rapidly on foolscap and thrown on the floor. Subsequently, with his foot, he would move them about, grouping together characters who would appear on the stage together, to judge if their colour and accent would be effective, and altering if the need arose." *Self-Portrait*, p. 369, note.

12.   Lillah McCarthy: *Myself and My Friends* (London: Butterworth, 1933), pp. 112-13.

13.   The various productions may be listed: (1) Stage Society, Globe Theatre, 1900; (2) Meyerhold production, designed by Sapounov, Studio Theatre, Moscow, 1905; (3) Lugné-Poe production, Théâtre des Maturins, Paris, 1906 and (4) Granville Barker production, designed by Ricketts, St. James's Theatre, London, 1912.

14.   Michael Kennedy, *The Works of Ralph Vaughan Williams* (London: Oxford, 1964), p. 468. The incidental music has not been published or recorded for public distribution. The unpublished manuscript is in the possession of Basil Ashmore.

15.   For example, Nikolaus Pevsner, *Pioneers of Modern Design* (Harmondsworth: Penguin, 1960), pp. 106-7.

16.   Thomas Howarth, *Charles Rennie Mackintosh and the Modern Movement* (London: Routledge, 1952). This study contains numerous illustrations of this type of design. Mackintosh's wife used her maiden name, Margaret MacDonald, for professional purposes.

17.   Ernest Short, *Theatrical Cavalcade* (London: Eyre & Spottiswoode, 1942), p. 183.

18.   Bottomley, "Charles Ricketts R.A.," pp. 392 and 381.

Chapter 4

1.   The Irish Literary Theatre, The Irish National Dramatic Company, The Irish National Theatre Society, The Abbey Company Limited are all various names used since 1899 by the group of players assembled under Yeats, Lady Gregory, Frank and Willie Fay (and later J.M. Synge). The group was popularly known as The Irish Players. See Lady Gregory, *Our Irish Theatre* (London: Putnam, 1913).

2.   Lionel Johnson, W.B. Yeats, Ernest Rhys, Herbert Horne, Selwyn Image, T.W. Rolleston, Ernest Dowson, John Davidson, Richard Le Gallienne, Francis Thompson, Arthur Symons and John Todhunter among others formed an association of poets and critics in 1891 known as The Rhymers' Club. They held meetings at a hostelry known as The Cheshire Cheese. See Joseph Hone, *W.B. Yeats, 1865-1939* (London: Macmillan, 1962), p. 78-79.

3.   W.B. Yeats, *Autobiographies* (London: Macmillan, 1955), p. 209. The fanaticism Yeats refers to might have been spiritualism or one of its associated religions which Ricketts would have disdained.

4.   W.B. Yeats, *The Letters of W.B. Yeats*, edited by Allan Wade (New York: Macmillan, 1955), p. 436.

5.   William Rothenstein, the lithographer, and Pamela Coleman Smith (called Pixie Smith) both, in their separate media, made early portraits of Yeats. T. Sturge Moore, better known as a poet and dramatist, also designed books and created several fine cover designs for Yeats' works; Elinor Monsell designed the Queen Maeve and wolfhound logograph which the Abbey Theatre still uses; Althea Gyles designed Yeats' first bookplate.

6.   Yeats, *Autobiographies*, p. 349. Lugné-Poe's production of *Ubu Roi* at the Hôtel Corneille broke into riot almost as soon as it began. It was scatalogical, antiestablishment, what would now be called absurdist, and parodied the fashionable symbolist plays, many of whose authors were in the audience. Artists like Yeats found themselves obliged to support the continuation of the production against the howls of the rioters, even though they surely found the material of the play unsympathetic. On an earlier visit to Paris in 1894, Yeats had seen the five-hour production of Villiers de l'Isle Adam's *Axël* which became a touchstone for the symbolist dramatists, having a temporary but profound influence on Maeterlinck and Yeats among others.

7.   *The Speaker*, 11 May 1901, quoted in Denis Bablet, *Edward Gordon Craig*, trans. Daphne Woodward (London: Heinemann, 1966), p. 45.

8.   Yeats, *Letters*, pp. 385-86 and 380.

9.   W.G. Fay, "The Poet and the Actor" in *Scattering Branches, Tribute to the Memory of W.B. Yeats*, ed. Stephen Gwynn (London: Macmillan, 1940), p. 133. This model should not be confused with the later one of Craig's screens which Yeats used after 1910 to plan the staging of his plays.

10.   Several photographs from the Holloway and Henderson collections, now in the National Library of Ireland, and from the private collection of Senator Michael Yeats are reproduced in James W. Flannery, *W.B. Yeats and the Idea of a Theatre* (New Haven: Yale University Press, 1976), following p. 200. See also W.B. Yeats's letter to Lady Gregory (21 January 1904): "I have written to Miss Horniman suggesting as delicately as I could that there ought not to be gorgeousness of costume." Yeats, *Letters*, p. 427.

11. W.B. Yeats, *W.B. Yeats & T. Sturge Moore: Their Correspondence: 1901-1937*, edited by Ursula Bridge (London: Routledge & Kegan Paul, 1953), pp. 5-6.

12. See Sylvia V. Eichen, "Costume in the Theatre of Edward Gordon Craig," Ph.D. diss., University of Toronto, 1977, pp. 109-10, and *Dido and Aeneas*, plate XIV.

13. Flannery, *Yeats and the Idea of a Theatre*, p. 257.

14. Liam Miller, *The Noble Drama of W.B. Yeats*, (Dublin: Dolmen, 1977), p. 111, fig. 26, and p. 156, fig. 39. Slightly larger measurements are given in Sean McCann, *The Story of the Abbey Theatre* (London: Four Square Books, 1967), p. 55, but these are not to be trusted, and the scale drawings in Miller's study settle the matter.

15. Flannery, *Yeats and the Idea of a Theatre*, p. 258: "I absolutely refuse to countenance any more makeshift stuff made up at the local oilshop."

16. Miller, *Noble Drama of Yeats*, p. 168.

17. Joseph Holloway, *Joseph Holloway's Abbey Theatre*, edited by Robert Hogan and Michael J. O'Neill (Carbondale: Southern Illinois University Press, 1967), p. 148. Holloway was the architect responsible for the conversion of the Abbey Theatre, but he is chiefly remembered for the collection of photographs, press cuttings and his own manuscript diaries recording the theatrical events of Dublin during his lifetime. His collection and diaries are now in the National Library of Ireland.

18. Quoted in James W. Flannery, "Gordon Craig and the Visual Arts of the Theatre," in *Yeats and the Theatre*, edited by Robert O'Driscoll and Lorna Reynolds (Toronto: Macmillan, 1975), p. 102.

19. W.B. Yeats, "The Play, The Player and the Scene," *Samhain*, Dec. 1904, p. 32.

20. Roland Barthes, *Critical Essays*, trans. Richard Howard (Evanston: Northwestern University Press, 1972), p. 42.

21. In a symposium "The Art of the Theatre," in *The New Age* (16 June 1910) reprinted in W.B. Yeats, *Uncollected Prose*, 2 vols., edited by John P. Frayne and Colton Johnson (London: Macmillan, 1975), II, p. 383. A.R. Orage conducted this symposium in his weekly paper *The New Age*. Shaw, Craig, Yeats and others each answered a number of set questions.

22. Ricketts offered to raise £600 so that Craig could mount a projected Stage Society production of Yeats's *The Countess Cathleen*. Craig ignored the offer.

23. J.M. Synge, *Plays*, edited by Ann Saddlemyer, III and IV of *Collected Works*, general editor Robin Skelton (London: Oxford, 1968), III, p. 119. Future reference to Synge's plays are indicated after each quotation by volume and page number, and refer to this edition.

24. Holloway, *Abbey Theatre*, p. 50, referring to the production of *On Baile's Strand* in December 1904 for which Miss Annie E.F. Horniman, patron of the theatre, had designed the costumes.

25. Yeats, "The Play, the Player and the Scene," p. 32.

26. Sydney Morgan was one of the actors in the early Abbey company, but the note does not appear to refer to him.

27. Quoted in Flannery, *Yeats and the Idea of a Theatre*, p. 260. The "Shawn" referred to is Seaghan Barlow, whom Lady Gregory is said to have had to instruct as to how to hold and apply a paintbrush. It is uncertain whether or not this set design was ever executed.

28.   Synge, *Collected Works: Plays*, IV, 54.

29.   For example, the decorative metalwork cover on the Shrine of St. Patrick's Bell, illustrated in *The Irish World*, edited by Brian de Breffny (London: Abrams, 1977), following p. 72, fig. 5.

30.   Sara Allgood, who played Lavarcham, would have been twenty-six. Her sister Molly, using the stage name Maire O'Neill, played Deirdre and codirected the play. She would have been twenty-two at this time.

31.   Lennox Robinson, "Irish Dramatic Costume" in *Robes of Thespis*, edited by Rupert Mason, George Sheringham and R. Boyd Morrison (London: Ernest Benn, 1928), p. 36: "We could afford to risk nothing, it was only by economy of the most bitter kind that we have managed to survive." Lennox Robinson replaced Synge as one of the directors of the Abbey Theatre. Yeats and Lady Gregory remained actively involved.

32.   The rippling effect depends upon the relative proportions of the contrasting lines, any small regular pattern using highly contrasting tones or values has this effect in movement, not unlike the scales of a leaping fish, or the lines on a television screen.

33.   A photograph identified as Maire O'Neill playing Deirdre of the Sorrows, 1910, is reproduced in J.M. Synge, *Letters to Molly*, edited by Ann Saddlemyer (Cambridge, Mass.: Harvard University Press, 1971), p. 319. She is shown wearing an old-fashioned costume of Greek inspiration, which is not the costume Ricketts designed. Ann Saddlemyer informs me that the first performance of this production was dressed in a mixture of some Ricketts costumes and some old stock. Ricketts' dress for Deirdre may not have been ready by the first performance. The costume in the photograph had been designed for an earlier Yeats play by Lady Gregory.

34.   Liam Miller, "W.B. Yeats and Stage Design at the Abbey Theatre," *Malahat Review* (No. 16, 1970), [plate 4] following p. 64.

35.   Letter, W.B. Yeats to Ricketts, 11 June 1914, in Ricketts, *Self-Portrait*, pp. 196-97.

36.   Ricketts, *Self-Portrait*, p. 203.

37.   Fay and Carswell, *The Fays of the Abbey Theatre*, p. 300. Frank Fay played Seanchan.

38.   W.B. Yeats, *The King's Threshold and On Baile's Strand* (London: A.H. Bullen, 1904), p. 25. Future references to the plays are indicated by page numbers from this edition, which I choose as the one most likely to have been used by Ricketts, though I have also consulted *The Variorum Edition of the Plays of W.B. Yeats*, edited by Russel K. Alspach and Catherine C. Alspach (New York: Macmillan, 1966). Though Yeats used the spelling Cuchullain in this 1904 edition, for the sake of consistency, I have used the spelling Cuchulain, which Yeats himself later preferred.

39.   See also Yeats' poem "To a poet who would have me praise certain bad poets, imitators of his and mine," in *Collected Poems* (London: Macmillan, 1950), p. 105.

40.   Yeats, *Collected Poems*, pp. 459-65.

41.   Mrs. Champion was the London dressmaker whom Ricketts had recommended to Lady Gregory. The same note is repeated on several of the rough working drawings.

42.   Ricketts, *Self-Portrait*, pp. 238-39.

43.   Ibid., p. 239. Obviously the company rehearsed at least parts of several plays but also had a costume parade or dress rehearsal for the revival of *On Baile's Strand*. The Lady Gregory play was probably *Shanwalla*, which was not favorably received, except by G.B. Shaw.

44. Yeats, *Variorum Plays*, p. 489, stage directions. Synge; *Letters to Molly*, p. 111 indicates that the introduction of the three women took place in production as early as 1907.

45. Robinson, "Irish Dramatic Costume," pp. 36-37.

46. Letter, Ricketts to Lillah McCarthy, [Sept. 1918], Ricketts Manuscripts, Humanities Research Center, University of Texas, Austin.

47. Ricketts, *Self-Portrait*, pp. 302-3.

48. It is interesting to note that, in our own times of budgetary restraints in theatre, there are signs of a return to Ricketts' idea of interchangeable stock costumes. The Royal Shakespeare Company recently mounted *Henry IV: Part I, Henry IV: Part II, Henry V* and *The Merry Wives of Windsor*, all designed by Abdel Farrah, using the same basic costumes throughout. At the Glasgow Citizens Theatre over the past several years Philip Prowse has staged a number of the Jacobean revenge tragedies using the same stock costumes for the various plays.

Chapter 5

1. Letter, G.B. Shaw to Ricketts, 8 July 1907, quoted in Ricketts, *Sixty-Five Illustrations*, [xvii].

2. For example, Charles Kean (1811-68) and his wife Ellen Tree (1806-80), actor-managers of the Princess' Theatre from 1851 through 1859, took great pains to present historically accurate, visually pleasing, often lavish productions. Charity performances for such organizations as the Red Cross were often given in afternoon performances for one or two occasions only. Actors and designers donated their time freely.

3. *The Admirable Crichton* by J.M. Barrie, Coliseum Theatre, 9 June 1916.

4. Gabrielle Enthoven (1868-1950), English theatre historian and collector of playbills, theatrical prints, programs, cuttings relating to London theatre. She presented this material to the Victoria and Albert Museum and the collection now bears her name.
    Mary Davis, wife of Sir Edmund Davis, the financier. The Davises were great collectors and patrons of the arts. Ricketts often advised them about purchasing paintings. They provided a home for Ricketts and Shannon and studio space for several artists. Ultimately, Ricketts and Shannon were given the Keep of Chilham Castle, the Davis' estate near Canterbury.
    Alice, Dowager Princess of Monaco (1858-1925) was a well-known hostess, both in Paris and in London. She stayed at Claridge's Hotel when in London and was famous for the luncheon parties at which she entertained artists, actors and musicians.
    Maria Appia, niece of the well-known design theorist Adolphe Appia, and wife of Thomas Sturge Moore.

5. McCarthy, *Myself and My Friends.*

6. William Poel (1852-1934), actor and director, founder of the English Stage Society in 1894, and innovator in the movement towards a return to the relative simplicity of Elizabethan staging of Shakespeare.
    Wilson Barrett (1847-1904), actor-manager, toured extensively in the United States, dominions and provinces, famous for his melodramatic roles.
    Sir Philip Ben Greet (1857-1936), actor-manager, toured especially in Shakespeare productions, providing a training for many young actors.
    Harley Granville Barker (later Granville-Barker), (1877-1946), playwright, actor, director in the vanguard of the new movement in the theatre during the early years of this century.

Married Lillah McCarthy in 1906. They were divorced in 1918 and he retired from the stage, with the one exception of his directing Maeterlinck's *The Betrothal* in 1921.

The Court Theatre, Sloane Square, Chelsea—remarkable for its series of new plays, especially those of George Bernard Shaw, during the management of J.E. Vedrenne and H. Granville Barker from 1904 through 1907.

7.   McCarthy, *Myself and My Friends,* p. 115.

8.   Ibid., p. 110.

9.   Ibid., pp. 220-21.

10.   The strange embargo which Granville Barker placed upon any mention of his name, or of their work together, after their divorce, gives a rather peculiar slant to her autobiography and is probably responsible, to some extent, for her lack of fame.

11.   Bennett later wrote the libretto for an opera, *Judith,* which had some success at Covent Garden. There has been some speculation that Ricketts designed this opera. He certainly did not, though Bennett had been delighted with the 1919 designs and recommended that Ricketts be given the designing of the opera.

12.   Thomas Sturge Moore, *Poems.* 2 vols., collected edition (London: Macmillan, 1933), II, 133. Future references are to volume and page of this edition.

13.   Arnold Bennett, *Judith: A Play in Three Acts* (London: Chatto & Windus, 1919), p. 67. Future references to the text are indicated by page references to this edition.

14.   Discussed above, p. 23.

15.   For example, Frederick L. Gwynn, *Sturge Moore and the Life of Art* (Lawrence: University of Kansas Press, 1951).

16.   The Swiss scenic designer Adolphe Appia whose theories on the use of theatrical lighting were particularly influential. See "Adolphe Appia—A Gospel for Modern Stages." *Theatre Arts Monthly,* 16 (1932), pp. 605-88.

17.   Unpublished letter, Ricketts to Michael Field, 9 April 1906, British Library MS. 58089.

18.   Unpublished letter, Ricketts to T. Sturge Moore, [December 1915], British Library MS. 58086.

19.   Unpublished letter, Ricketts to T. Sturge Moore, [December 1915], British Library MS. 58086.

20.   For example, Anne Yeats' setting for her father's play *Purgatory,* Abbey Theatre, Dublin, 1938, described in Miller, *Noble Drama of Yeats,* pp. 306-7.

21.   Arnold Dolmetsch (1858-1940), musician who recreated early musical instruments and stimulated interest in medieval music. See Margaret Campbell, *Dolmetsch: The Man and his Work* (London: Hamish Hamilton, 1977).

Florence Farr (1864-1917) actress and innovator, associated with both Shaw and Yeats. Her experiments with chanting verse to Dolmetsch's psaltery were not entirely successful because she was not "an executive musician." (Campbell, *Dolmetsch,* p. 144, n. 18). See Josephine Johnson, *Florence Farr: Bernard Shaw's "New Woman"* (Gerrard's Cross: Colin Smythe, 1975).

Edmund Dulac (1882-1953) close friend of Yeats and of Ricketts; book illustrator and theatrical designer, also experimented with instrumental music accompanied by chanting verse, and composed music as well as designed masks and costumes for Yeats. See Colin White, *Edmund Dulac* (London: Studio Vista, 1976).

22.   Michael Field went so far as to describe one such experiment as "toothache calling unto toothache." (Campbell, *Dolmetsch,* p. 45).

23.   Ibid., p. 144.

24.   Ricketts' letters and diaries give full testimony to his deep love of music. However, he did not compose the opera *Näil* as claimed by Frederick L. Gwynn, *Sturge Moore and the Life of Art.* Ricketts designed the opera, Covent Garden, July 1919; the music was composed by his friend Isidore de Lara.

25.   Unpublished letter, T. Sturge Moore to Ricketts, [January 1916], British Library MS. 58086.

26.   Ricketts, *Self-Portrait,* p. 253.

27.   Arnold Bennett, *The Journals of Arnold Bennett (1911-1921)* 3 vols., edited by Newman Flower (London: Cassell, 1932), II, p. 243. Lillah McCarthy married the Professor Keeble referred to. He was later knighted for his service to botany.

28.   Claude Lovat Fraser (1890-1921) graphic and theatrical designer, friend of Ricketts.

29.   Bennett, *Journals,* II, pp. 246-47.

30.   McCarthy, *Myself and My Friends,* p. 229.

31.   Bennett, *Journals,* II, pp. 248-49.

32.   Ibid., II, p. 250.

33.   Thomas Hardy's *The Dynasts* was performed in a very much abbreviated form, edited and directed by Granville Barker at the Kingsway Theatre, November 1914. Ricketts designed the production.

34.   McCarthy, *Myself and My Friends,* p. 202. She refers to Masefield's *Philip the King* at Covent Garden, November 1914, designed by Ricketts.

35.   *Chu Chin Chow,* His Majesty's Theatre, 1914 for a run of 2,238 performances.

36.   McCarthy, *Myself and My Friends,* p. 230.

37.   The photographs have obviously been taken in a studio and not on the set.

38.   McCarthy, *Myself and My Friends,* p. 230.

39.   For example, the throne room scene in Maeterlinck's *The Betrothal,* Gaiety Theatre, January 1921, (fig. 39).

40.   Ricketts was an acknowledged expert on Eastern art. In particular he collected Persian miniatures, many of which are now in the Fitzwilliam Museum, Cambridge. In tribute to Ricketts' and Shannon's knowledge in this field Edmund Dulac painted an exquisite pastiche in the form of a Persian miniature depicting Ricketts and Shannon as Hindu gods. This is reproduced in Colin White's *Edmund Dulac,* p. 68, plate 41. Unfortunately the text is confused in that it states that Ricketts is shown holding a tiny scroll celebrating his election as an associate of the Royal Academy. In fact it is Shannon who is shown holding the scroll. Shannon was awarded the A.R.A. in 1911, the full R.A. in 1921. Ricketts did not receive his A.R.A. till 1922, his R.A. till 1928.

41.   McCarthy, *Myself and My Friends,* p. 230.

42.   Bennett, *Journals,* II, pp. 249-50. Joseph Darracott, *The World of Charles Ricketts* (New York: Methuen, 1980) states that the dress was censored by the Lord Chamberlain, p. 180.

43. Ricketts, *Sixty-Five Illustrations*, plate LV.

44. Léon Bakst (1866-1924), the most famous of a group of designers which also included Alexandre Benois and Natalie Goncharova, associated with the impresario Serge de Diaghilev, at first in a St. Petersburg art magazine *Mir Isskustva* (World of Art), later in organizing exhibitions of Russian art and tours of the *Ballets Russes* to Paris and London, beginning such tours in 1909. It is interesting to note that Bakst and Ricketts were exactly the same age.

45. For example, Flaubert, *Salammbô* (1862), Edward Fitzgerald's version of *Rubaiyat of Omâr Khayam* (1859), Richard Burton's translation of *Arabian Nights* (1855-88) and, in painting, Ingres' *Odalisque*, Delacroix' *Massacre à Chios* (1824), and Gustave Moreau's whole series of paintings of Salome.

46. Ricketts' knowledge of the East was strengthened by visits to Greece, Egypt and North Africa. He was frequently called in by museums to authenticate works of art. He records that the famous dealer and collector Ready, "the only man whose insight I feared," complimented him shortly before Ready's death by telling him: "After all, no one in London has your knowledge." *Self-Portrait*, p. 186.

47. Charles Spencer, *Léon Bakst* (New York: St. Martin's Press, 1973), p. 70.

48. Ricketts, *Self-Portrait*, p. 204.

49. Ibid., pp. 174-75.

50. Spencer, *Bakst*, p. 105, quoting from the records of the Fine Art Society.

51. The book was Arsene Alexandre's *The Decorative Art of Léon Bakst* (London: Fine Art Society, 1913). Ricketts offered to lend it to the Bottomleys (*Self-Portrait*, p. 182).

52. Unpublished postcard, Ricketts to Lillah McCarthy, [1912, from Egypt], Humanities Research Center, University of Texas, Austin.

53. Ricketts, *Self-Portrait*, p. 176.

54. Ibid., pp. 177-78 (letter to the painter William Anthony Pye, 1912).

55. Ibid., p. 227 (letter to Gordon Bottomley, 4 January 1915).

56. Spencer, *Bakst*, p. 150.

57. James Laver, *The Concise History of Costume and Fashion* (New York: Abrams, 1969), p. 225.

58. Osbert Lancaster, *Homes Sweet Homes*, 3rd ed. (London: John Murray 1963), p. 56.

59. White, *Dulac*, pp. 23-35. Originally exhibited Leicester Galleries, 1907.

60. Spencer, Bakst, p. 215.

Chapter 6

1. Barker had been engaged to direct this production before he retired from active involvement in the theatre. Any further theatrical involvement was in an advisory capacity.

2. Ricketts, *Self-Portrait*, p. 331.

3. Among other statements which created public hostility to Shaw was his review of Cecil Chesterton's tract *The Perils of Peace*. The review, published in *New Republic*, 6 January 1917, pp. 270-76, under the title "On British Squealing, and the Situation After the War,"

stated that British stoicism had been badly shaken by German methods of war. The question of Shaw's reactions to war is discussed in Stanley Weintraub's *Journey to Heartbreak: The Crucible Years of Bernard Shaw* (New York: Weybright & Talley, 1971), pp. 194-95.

4.   Ibid., p. 329.

5.   William Poel, *What is Wrong with the Stage* (London: Allen and Unwin, 1920), pp. 9-10, quoted in Margery M. Morgan, *The Shavian Playground* (London: Methuen, 1974), p. 238, n. 1.

6.   Morgan, *The Shavian Playground*, pp. 248-49. Martin Meisel, *Shaw and the Nineteenth Century Theater* (Princeton: Princeton University Press, 1963) makes another comparison between *Saint Joan* and nineteenth century martyr plays which were popular star vehicles for touring actresses, pp. 365-70.

7.   Sybil Thorndike, quoting Maude Roydon in Elizabeth Sprigge, *Sybil Thorndike Casson* (London: Gollantz, 1971), p. 159.

8.   A copy of the original program is in the Enthoven Collection at the Victoria and Albert Museum, London.

9.   Jack Hawkins, *Anything for a Quiet Life: An Autobiography* (London: Hamish Hamilton, 1973), p. 20.

10.   George Bernard Shaw, *Saint Joan*, preface, p. 75. I refer to *Collected Plays with their Prefaces*, edited by Dan H. Laurence (London: Max Reinhardt, the Bodley Head, 1970), vol. 6.

11.   Gordon Gow, "Nostalgia for the Vanishing Proscenium," *Plays and Players*, 25 (July 1978), pp. 8-9.

12.   *Saint Joan* by Bernard Shaw with stage settings and sketches by C. Ricketts, numbered edition (London: Constable, 1924). This edition sold slowly in Britain but more successfully in North America.

13.   Ricketts, "The Art of Stage Decoration," p. 246.

14.   Sir Edmund and Lady Davis gave Ricketts and Shannon the old Keep in the grounds of Chilham Castle to use as a country retreat.

15.   Raymond Mander and Joe Mitchenson, *Theatrical Companion to Shaw* (London: Rockliff, 1954), p. 209.

16.   Daniel C. Gerould, "*Saint Joan* in Paris," *The Shaw Review*, 7 (January 1964), pp. 11-23.

17.   In 1833 Alexandre de Sommerard established this museum in an old Cluniac monastery to display the history of medieval French civilization as reflected in its paintings, tapestries, pottery and furniture. It was the first museum of its kind, predating the larger South Kensington Museum, London (now the Victoria and Albert Museum) by twenty years.

18.   For example, the paintings of Jean Fouquet (1415-85). Fouquet painted a Madonna with the features of Agnes Sorel, the king's mistress. The king was Charles VII, the dauphin of *Saint Joan*. The painting is now in the Koningklijk Museum, Antwerp.

19.   The paintings of the prayer book have been frequently reproduced. One such example is in *Larousse Encyclopedia of Byzantine and Medieval Art*, general editor Rene Huyghe (New York: Prometheus Press, 1963), plate facing p. 352.

20.   Directed by Laurence Olivier, produced by J. Arthur Rank, 1946.

21. Winston became a friend of Ricketts and Ricketts often suggested him to actors in need of a costumer, after they had worked together on *Saint Joan.* Winston also helped make costumes for the *Macbeth* and *Henry VIII* which Ricketts designed. Not least of his commendations was that he was happy to be paid in chocolates, which may have had something to do with his great bulk.

22. Leighton House, part of which has been used as the temporary location of the British Theatre Museum, a branch of the Victoria and Albert Museum.

23. Sprigge, *Sybil Thorndike Casson*, p. 164.

24. Private interview.

25. Letter, G.B. Shaw to Lawrence Langner, codirector of the New York Theatre Guild (1923), quoted in "The New York Critics and *Saint Joan*," *The Shaw Bulletin*, 1 (January 1955), p. 10.

26. A.B. Walkley, *The Times* (27 March 1924) quoted in *Shaw: The Critical Heritage*, edited by T.F. Evans (London: Routledge & Kegan Paul, 1976), p. 287.

27. The production relied heavily upon pageantry and masque for which Ricketts' amber tones, as if lit by candles, were considered very appropriate.

28. Dame Sybil later admitted to her family that the role simply escaped her.

29. Norman Wilkinson designed sets for Granville Barker, particularly famous for *The Winter's Tale* (1912) and *A Midsummer Night's Dream* (1914).

    Albert Rutherston, brother of William Rotherstein, who adopted this version of the name. He often collaborated with Wilkinson. Designed Shaw's *Androcles and the Lion* for Barker, 1913.

    George Sheringham, designed for Nigel Playfair at the Lyric Hammersmith, notably *The Duenna* (1924) and *Love in a Village* (1928). Along with Ricketts he remounted the Gilbert and Sullivan operas for D'Oyly Carte after 1928.

    Aubrey Hammond, designed for Walter Bridge-Adams at the Stratford Memorial Theatre, Stratford-upon-Avon, England.

    Tanya Moiseiwitsch, designed at Stratford-upon-Avon, The Abbey Theatre, Dublin, The Old Vic, the National Theatre and at Stratford, Ontario. Like Ricketts, in *Saint Joan* she is frequently concerned with the use of semipermanent fixed units combined with stylized historical adjuncts brought on and off quickly for continuity and speed in pageant or chronicle plays.

    Motley (Sophie Harris, Margaret Harris and Elizabeth Montgomery) designed Shakespeare and historical plays, notably Gordon Daviot's *Richard of Bordeaux* (1932) for John Gielgud.

Chapter 7

1. Ricketts, "The Art of Stage Decoration," p. 246.

2. There was some German interest and at least talk of a possibility of Ricketts' designs being used at Bayreuth, which came to nothing. Ricketts, *Self-Portrait,* p. 349.

3. L.P. Rosenberg, 38 Avenue de l'Opéra, Paris published a catalogue (1-30 June 1909), of Hok'sai and Holkei from the collection of Ricketts and Shannon.

4. Letter, Ricketts to Rupert d'Oyly Carte, quoted in *The Gilbert and Sullivan,* a catalogue of the Prints, Photographs and Models of the Operas and their Authors, (London: Whitbread &

Co., Ltd., [n.d.]). The Gilbert and Sullivan is a public house on John Adams Street, London which contains several Gilbert and Sullivan exhibits.

5.   Alan Jefferson, "Notes and Queries—Charles Ricketts." *Theatre Notebook.* 22 (1963), p. 131.

6.   Ricketts, *Self-Portrait,* p. 396.

7.   Ibid., pp. 367-68.

8.   Joseph Darracott, *The World of Charles Ricketts* p. 117, suggests that Ricketts' interest in stage sets and props was one of the motives for his lifelong habit of collecting antiquities and *objets d'art,* even broken objects.

9.   Unpublished letter, Ricketts to Charles H. Shannon, 24 November 1927. British Library MS. 58085.

10.   Ricketts, *Self-Portrait,* p. 370.

11.   Victoria and Albert Museum, Dept. of Prints and Drawings, Press No. 92D33.

12.   W.B. Yeats, *On the Boiler,* quoted in John Unterecker, *Reader's Guide to William Butler Yeats* (New York: Noonday Press, 1959), p. 286.

13.   William Archer and Harley Granville Barker, *A National Theatre Scheme and Estimates* (London: Duckworth, 1907).

14.   The final irony is that Ricketts was one of the moving spirits behind the establishment of the National Arts-Collection Fund.

15.   William Rothenstein, *Men and Memories: Recollections,* 3 vols. (London: Faber & Faber, 1931-39), I, pp. 174-76.

16.   Ibid., III, p. 162, quoting a letter from Manning.

17.   Sir Charles Holmes, "Review of *Charles Ricketts, R.A.: Sixty-five Illustrations,*" *Burlington Magazine.* 62 (1933), pp. 247-48.

18.   Perhaps because of recent austerities and calculated publicity about the lavish Tudor costumes in *Elizabeth of England,* queues for tickets formed days before the box office opened.

19.   Ricketts, *Self-Portrait,* pp. 368-69, n. 1.

Bibliography

Unpublished Manuscripts

British Library Manuscript Acquisitions 58085-58118, Ricketts and Shannon materials, 34 vols., presented by Mrs. Maria Sturge Moore and family.

58085	Correspondence, Ricketts and Shannon
58086	Correspondence, Ricketts and T. Sturge Moore
58087-89	Correspondence, Ricketts, Shannon and Michael Field
58090-91	Correspondence, Ricketts and various correspondents
58092-93	Literary Papers
58098	Ricketts' Diary, 1900
58099	Ricketts' Diary, 1901
58100	Ricketts' Diary, 1902
58101	Ricketts' Diary, 1903
58102	Ricketts' Diary, 1904
58103	Ricketts' Diary, 1905
58104	Ricketts' Diary, 1906
58105	Ricketts' Diary, 1914
58106	Ricketts' Diary, 1915
58107	Ricketts' Diary, 1916
58108	Ricketts' Diary, 1917
58109	Ricketts' Diary, 1918
58110	Shannon's Diary, 1898
58118	Shannon's Diary, 1906

British Library Manuscript Acquisitions 45851-52, Michael Field Papers.

Ricketts' Manuscripts, Humanities Research Center, University of Texas, Austin, Texas, Correspondence, Ricketts to Lillah McCarthy

Ricketts' Manuscripts, Beinecke Rare Book Room and Manuscript Library, Yale University, New Haven, Connecticut. Correspondence, Ricketts to John Grey, Oscar Killman.

Books and Articles

Abbey Theatre, *Stage Designs for the Abbey Theatre.* Exhibition catalogue, Peacock Theatre, Dublin, 1967.

Abercrombie, Lascelles. *Poetry, its Music and Meaning.* London: Oxford University Press, 1932.

Acton, Harold. *Memoirs of an Aesthete.* London: Methuen, 1948.

Adam, Phillippe Auguste Villiers de l'Isle. *Axël.* Translated by June Guicharnaud. Englewood Cliffs: Prentice-Hall, 1970.

"Adolphe Appia—A Gospel for Modern Stages." An entire issue of *Theatre Arts Monthly* devoted to Appia. 16 (1932), 605-88.

Agate, James. "Oscar Wilde and the Theatre." *The Masque,* no. 3 (Dec. 1946), reprinted in *The Masque Library.* London: The Curtain Press, 1950.

————. *Red Letter Nights.* London: Jonathan Cape, 1944.

————. *A Short View of the English Stage, 1900-1926.* London: Herbert Jenkins, 1926.

Alexandre, Arsene. *The Decorative Art of Léon Bakst.* London: Fine Art Society, 1913.

Appia, Adolphe. *Music & the Art of the Theatre.* Edited by Bernard Hewitt and translated by Robert W. Corrigan and Mary Douglas Dirks. Coral Gables: University of Miami Press, 1962.

Archer, William. *The Old Drama and the New.* New York: Dodd, Mead & Co., 1929.

———— and Harley Granville Barker, *A National Theatre Scheme and Estimates.* London: Duckworth, 1907.

Archibald, Douglas. *Yeats.* Syracuse: Syracuse University Press, 1983.

Ashwell, Lena. *Myself a Player.* London: Michael Joseph, 1936.

Bablet, Denis. *Edward Gordon Craig.* Translated by Daphne Woodward. London: Heinemann, 1966.

————. *Esthétique Général du Décor de Théâtre de 1870 à 1914.* Paris: Centre National de la Recherche Scientifique, 1965.

Barker, Felix. *The House that Stoll Built: The Story of the Coliseum Theatre.* London: Frederick Muller, 1957.

Barthes, Roland. "The Disease of Costume," in *Critical Essays.* Translated by Richard Howard. Evanston: Northwestern University Press, 1972.

Beerbohm, Max. *Around Theatres.* 2 vols. London: Heinemann, 1924.

————. *Last Theatres, 1904-1910.* London: Rupert Hart-Davis, 1970.

Bennett, Arnold. *The Journals of Arnold Bennett.* 3 vols. Edited by Newman Flower. London: Cassell, 1932.

————. *Judith: A Play in Three Acts.* London: Chatto & Windus, 1919.

Berst, Charles A. *Bernard Shaw and the Art of Drama.* Urbana: University of Illinois, 1973.

Blanche, Jacques-Emile. *Portraits of a Lifetime, 1870-1914.* Edited by Walter Clement, introduction by Harley Granville Barker. London: Dent, 1937.

Block, Haskell M. *Mallarmé and the Symbolist Drama.* Detroit: Wayne State University Press, 1963.

Bottomley, Gordon. "Charles Ricketts, R.A." *Theatre Arts Monthly,* 16 (1932), 377-90.

————. *Poet & Painter: Correspondence between Gordon Bottomley and Paul Nash (1910-1946).* Edited by Claude Collier Abbott and Anthony Bertram. London: Oxford University Press, 1955.

————. *A Stage for Poetry: My Purposes with my Plays.* Kendal: Titus Wilson, 1948.

Bradbrook, Muriel C. *English Dramatic Form: A History of its Development.* London: Chatto & Windus, 1965.

Brown, Ivor. *Parties of the Play.* London: Ernest Benn, 1924.

Calloway, Stephen. *Charles Ricketts: subtle and fantastic decorator.* London: Thames and Hudson, 1979.

_____ and Paul Delaney. *Charles Ricketts and Charles Shannon: an aesthetic partnership* (catalogue of an exhibition at Orleans House, Twickenham). Richmond: London Borough of Richmond upon Thames, 1979.

Campbell, Margaret. *Dolmetsch: The Man and his Work*. London: Hamish Hamilton, 1975.

Carter, Huntley. *The New Spirit in Drama and Art*. London: Palmer, 1912.

_____. *The New Spirit in the European Theatre, 1914-1924*. London: Benn, 1925.

Casson, John. *Lewis & Sybil, a Memoir*. London: Collins, 1972.

Chamberlin, J.E. *Ripe was the Drowsy Hour: the Age of Oscar Wilde*. New York: Seabury Press, 1977.

Cheney, Sheldon. *The Art Theatre*. New York: Knopf, 1917.

_____. *The New Movement in the Theatre*. New York: Mitchell Kennerley, 1914.

_____. *Stage Decoration*. London: Chapman & Hall, 1923.

Clark, Kenneth. *Another Part of the Wood*. London: John Murray, 1977.

Courtney, W.L. *The Development of Maurice Maeterlinck*. London: Grant Richards, 1904.

Coxhead, Elizabeth. *Lady Gregory: A Literary Portrait*. London: Macmillan, 1961.

Craig, Edward Anthony. "Gordon Craig and Hubert van Herkomer." *Theatre Research* 10 (1969), 7-16.

_____. *Gordon Craig: The Story of his Life*. New York: Knopf, 1968.

Craig, Gordon. *On the Art of the Theatre*. 2nd ed. London: Heinemann, 1929.

Crompton, Louis. *Shaw the Dramatist*. Lincoln: University of Nebraska Press, 1969.

Crosse, Gordon. *Fifty Years of Shakespearean Playgoing*. London: Mowbray, 1940.

Darlington, W.A. *Six Thousand and One Nights: Fifty Years a Critic*. London: Harrap, 1960.

Darracott, Joseph. *All for Art: The Ricketts and Shannon Collection* (catalogue of an exhibition at the Fitzwilliam Museum, Cambridge). Cambridge: Fitzwilliam Museum, 1979.

_____. *The World of Charles Ricketts*. New York: Methuen, 1980.

Davenport, Millia. *The Book of Costume*. New York: Crown, 1948.

The Dictionary of National Biography, Supplement 1931-1940. Edited by L.G. Wickham Legg. London: Oxford University Press, 1949.

Donoghue, Denis. *The Third Voice: Modern British and American Verse Drama*. London: Oxford University Press, 1959.

Dukes, Ashley. *Elizabeth of England* by Frederick Bruckner, adapted from the German by Ashley Dukes. London: Ernest Benn, 1931.

Dukore, Bernard F. *Bernard Shaw, Director*. London: George Allen & Unwin, 1971.

_____. *Bernard Shaw, Playwright*. Columbia, University of Missouri Press, 1973.

Eichen, Sylvia V. "Costume in the Theatre of Edward Gordon Craig." Ph.D. diss., University of Toronto, 1977.

Ellis-Fermor, Una. *The Irish Dramatic Movement*. London: Methuen, 1939.

Engelberg, Edward. *The Vast Design: Pattern in W.B. Yeats' Aesthetics*. Toronto: University of Toronto Press, 1964.

Ervine, St. John. *The Theatre in my Time*. London: Rich & Cowan, 1933.

Fay, William G. and Catherine Carswell. *The Fays of the Abbey Theatre*. London: Rich and Cowan, 1935.

Field, Michael. *Work and Days: Extracts from the Journals of Michael Field*. Edited by T. Sturge Moore and D.C. Sturge Moore. London: John Murray, 1933.

Findlater, Richard. *Banned: A Review of Theatrical Censorship in Britain*. London: McGibbon & Kee, 1967.

_____. *The Player Queens*. London: Weidenfeld & Nicholson, 1976.

Fischel, Oscar. *Das Modern Buhnenbild*. Berlin: Wasmuth A-G. [1923].

Flannery, James W. "Gordon Craig and the Visual Arts of the Theatre," in *Yeats and the Theatre*. Edited by Robert O'Driscoll and Lorna Reynolds. Toronto: Macmillan, 1975.

————. *W.B. Yeats and the Idea of a Theatre.* New Haven: Yale University Press, 1976.

Fletcher, Iain and Frank Kermode, eds. *Poets of the Nineties.* London: John Baker, 1965.

Fletcher, Kyrle Ifan. "Charles Ricketts and the Theatre." *Theatre Notebook* 22 (1967), 6-23 and 6 illustrations.

Fraser, Grace Lovat. *In the Days of My Youth.* London: Cassell, 1970.

Fry, Roger. *Letters.* 2 vols. Edited by Denys Sutton. London: Chatto & Windus, 1972.

Fuerst, Walter Rene and Samuel J. Hume. *Twentieth Century Stage Decoration.* 2 vols. New York: Dover reprint, 1967.

Gascoigne, Bamber. *Twentieth Century Drama.* London: Hutchinson, 1962.

Gaunt, William. *The Aesthetic Adventure.* London: Jonathan Cape, 1945.

Gerould, Daniel C. "*Saint Joan* in Paris." *The Shaw Review.* 7 (1964), 11-23.

Gielgud, John. *Early Stages.* London: Macmillan, 1939.

Gide, André. *Journals: 1889-1939.* Paris: Gallimard, 1948.

The Gilbert and Sullivan. Catalogue of Prints, Photographs and Models of the Operas and their Authors. London: Whitbread & Co., Ltd., [n.d.].

Gilman, Richard. "The Special Quality of Joan," in *Common and Uncommon Masks: Writings on Theatre, 1961-1970.* New York: Random House, 1971, pp. 64-67.

Goncharova, Nathalie, with Michel Larionov and Pierre Vorms. *Les Ballets Russes: Serge de Diaghilev et la Décoration Théâtrale.* Paris: Dordogne, 1955.

Gray, Camille. *The Russian Experiment in Art: 1863-1922.* London: Thames & Hudson, 1962.

Gregory, Isabella Augusta (Lady). *Our Irish Theatre.* London: Putman, 1913.

Griffin, Alice. "The New York Critics and *Saint Joan.*" *The Shaw Bulletin* 1 (1955), 10-15.

Gwynn, Frederick L. *Sturge Moore and the Life of Art.* Lawrence: University of Kansas Press, 1951.

Gwynn, Stephen, ed. *Scattering Branches: Tribute to the Memory of W.B. Yeats.* London: Macmillan, 1940.

Halls, W.D. *Maurice Maeterlinck.* London: Oxford University Press, 1960.

Hartnoll, Phyllis, ed. *The Oxford Companion to the Theatre.* 3rd ed. London: Oxford University Press, 1967.

Hawkins, Jack. *Anything for a Quiet Life: an Autobiography.* London: Hamish Hamilton, 1973.

Henn, T.R. *The Harvest of Tragedy.* London: Methuen, 1956.

Hewison, Robert. *John Ruskin: The Argument of the Eye.* Princeton: Princeton University Press, 1976.

Hok'sai and Holkei in the Possession of Charles Ricketts and Charles H. Shannon. Catalogue. L.P. Rosenberg, 38 Avenue de l'Opera, Paris, 1-30 June 1909.

Hollander, Ann. *Seeing Through Clothes.* New York: Viking, 1975.

Holloway, Joseph. *Joseph Holloway's Abbey Theatre.* Edited by Robert Hogan and Michael J. O'Neil. Carbondale: Southern Illinois University Press, 1967.

Holmes, C.J. *Self & Partners (Mostly Self).* London: Constable, 1936.

Hone, Joseph M. *W.B. Yeats, 1865-1939.* London: Macmillan, 1965.

Hough, Graham. *The Last Romantics.* London: Duckworth, 1961.

Howarth, Thomas. *Charles Rennie Mackintosh and the Modern Movement.* London: Routledge, 1952.

Huysmans, Joris-Karl. *A Rebours.* Paris: G. Cres, 1922.

International Federation of Theatre Research. *Anatomy of an Illusion: Studies in Nineteenth Century Scene Design.* Amsterdam: Schetama & Holkema, 1969.

Irving, Laurence. "Review of Richard Southern's *Changeable Scenery.*" *Theatre Notebook* 6 (Oct. 1951-July 1952), 79.

Jackson, Holbrook. *The Eighteen Nineties, A Review of Art and Ideas at the Close of the Nineteenth Century.* New York: Kennerley, 1914.

Jasper, Gertrude R. *Adventure in the Theatre: Lugné-Poe and the Théâtre de l'Oeuvre.* New Brunswick: Rutgers University Press, 1947.

Jefferson, Alan. "Notes and Queries—Charles Ricketts." *Theatre Notebook* 22 (1963), 131.

Johnson, Josephine. *Florence Farr: Bernard Shaw's "New Woman."* Gerrard's Cross: Colin Smythe, 1975.

Jullian, Philippe. *Dreamers of Decadence: Symbolist painters of the 1890s.* Translated by Robert Baldick. New York: Praeger, 1975.

_____. *Oscar Wilde.* Translated by Violet Wyndham. London: Constable, 1969.

Kennet, Kathleen Bruce Scott (Lady). *Self-Portrait of an Artist.* London: John Murray, 1949.

Komisarjevsky, Theodore. *The Costume of the Theatre.* New York: Henry Holt, 1932.

Lancaster, Osbert. *Homes Sweet Homes.* 3rd ed. London: John Murray, 1963.

Laver, James. *The Concise History of Costume and Fashion.* New York: Abrams, [1969].

_____. *Costume in the Theatre.* New York: Hill and Wang, 1965.

_____. *Drama: Its Costume and Decor.* London: Studio Publications, 1951.

Le Gallienne, Richard. *The Romantic '90s.* London: Putnam, 1951.

Leeper, Janet. *Edward Gordon Craig—Designs for the Theatre.* Harmondsworth: Penguin Books, 1948.

Legge, Sylvia. *Affectionate Cousins: T. Sturge Moore and Maria Appia.* Oxford: Oxford University Press, 1980.

Lehmann, Andrew G. *The Symbolist Aesthetics in France: 1885-1895.* Oxford: Blackwell, 1950.

Lewis, Cecil. *Never Look Back: An Attempt at Autobiography.* London: Hutchinson, 1974.

McCarthy, Desmond. *The Court Theatre, 1904-1907: A Commentary and Criticism.* Edited by Stanley Weintraub. Coral Gables: University of Miami Press, 1966. (Books of the Theatre Series.)

McCarthy, Lillah. *Myself and My Friends.* London: Butterworth, 1933.

MacGowan, Kenneth. *The Theatre of Tomorrow.* London: Fisher Unwin, 1923.

Maeterlinck, Maurice. *Three Plays.* Introduced by Harley Granville Barker [translated by Alfred Sutro]. London: Gowans & Grey, 1911.

Mander, Raymond and Joe Mitchenson. *A Picture History of Gilbert and Sullivan.* London: Vista Books, 1962.

_____. *Theatrical Companion to Shaw; a Pictorial Record of the First Performances of the Plays of George Bernard Shaw.* London: Rockliff, 1954.

Meisel, Martin. *Shaw and the Nineteenth Century Theater.* Princeton: Princeton University Press, 1963.

Miller, Anna Irene. *The Independent Theatre in Europe: 1887 to the Present.* New York: Long & Smith, 1951.

Miller, Liam. *The Noble Drama of W.B. Yeats.* Dublin: Dolmen, 1977.

_____. "W.B. Yeats and Stage Design at the Abbey Theatre." *Malahat Review* 16 (1970), 50-64 and 17 illustrations.

Moore, George A. *Hail and Farewell: Ave, Salve, and Vale.* 3 vols. London: Heinemann, 1911-14.

Moore, Thomas Sturge. *Poems.* Collected edition, 2 vols. London: Macmillan, 1933.

Morgan, Margery M. *The Shavian Playground.* London: Methuen, 1974.

Morley, Sheridan. *Sybil Thorndike: A Life in the Theatre,* with a preface by Sir John Gielgud. London: Weidenfeld & Nicolson, 1977.

Morris, William. *Selected Writings and Designs.* Edited by Asa Briggs. Harmondsworth: Penguin, 1962.

Moses, Montrose J. *Maurice Maeterlinck: A Study.* New York: Duffield, 1911.

Moussinac, Léon. *The New Movement in the Theatre,* with an introduction by R.H. Packham and a foreword by Gordon Craig. New York: Benjamin Blom, 1932.

Murray, Gilbert. *Gilbert Murray: An Unfinished Autobiography.* Edited by Jean Smith and Arnold Toynbee. London: Allen & Unwin, 1960.

Nathan, Leonard E. *The Tragic Drama of William Butler Yeats: Figures in a Dance.* New York: Columbia University Press, 1965.

Nic Shiubhlaigh, Máire and Edward Kenny. *The Splendid Years.* Dublin: James Dugby, 1955.
Nicoll, Allandyce. *English Drama, 1900-1930.* Cambridge: Cambridge University Press.
O'Driscoll, Robert and Lorna Reynolds, eds. *Yeats and the Theatre.* Toronto: Macmillan, 1975.
Orme, Michael [Mrs. Alix A. Grein]. *J. T. Grein: The Story of a Pioneer, 1862-1935.* London: John Murray, 1936.
Peacock, Ronald. *The Poet in the Theatre.* New York: Hill and Wang, 1960.
Pearson, Hesketh. *George Bernard Shaw.* London: Collins, 1942.
————. *The Last Actor-Managers.* London: Methuen, 1950.
Pevsner, Nikolaus. *Pioneers of Modern Design.* Harmondsworth: Penguin, 1960.
Polunin, Vladimir. *The Continental Method of Scene Painting.* London: Beaumont, 1927.
Priestley, J.B. *The Edwardians.* London: Heinemann, 1972.
Purdom, C.B. *Harley Granville Barker: Man of the Theatre, Dramatist and Scholar.* London: Rockcliff, 1955.
Reynolds, Ernest. *Modern English Drama.* Norman, Oklahoma: University of Oklahoma Press, 1951.
Reynolds, Simon. "Sir Edmund Davis, Collector and Patron of the Arts." *Apollo* 111 (June 1980), 459-63.
Ricketts, Charles. *The Art of the Prado.* London: Hamilton, 1927.
————. *Beyond the Threshold,* by Jean Paul Raymond [pseudonym of Charles Ricketts], translated from the French and illustrated by Charles Ricketts. Printed privately: Plastrow, 1929.
————. *A Bibliography of the Books Issued by Hacon and Ricketts at the Vale Press.* London: Ballantyne, 1914.
————. *Charles Ricketts R.A.: Sixty-Five Illustrations.* Introduced by T. Sturge Moore. London: Cassell, 1932.
————. *Michael Field: A Memoir.* Edited by Paul Delaney. Edinburgh: Tragara Press, 1976.
————. *Pages From a Diary in Greece.* Edited by Paul Delaney. Edinburgh: Tragara Press, 1978.
————. *Pages on Art.* London: Constable, 1913.
————. *Saint Joan,* by Bernard Shaw, with the Stage Settings and Sketches by C. Ricketts. Numbered edition, London: Constable, 1924.
————. *Self-Portrait: Letters and Journals of Charles Ricketts.* Compiled by T. Sturge Moore, and edited by Cecil Lewis. London: Peter Davis, 1939.
————. *Shakespeare's Heroines.* [A souvenir of a series of performances given by the B.B.C. with illustrations by Charles Ricketts.] [London: B.B.C., 1926].
————. *Some Recollections of Oscar Wilde,* by Jean Paul Raymond [pseudonym of Charles Ricketts] and Charles Ricketts. London: Nonesuch Press, 1932.
————. *Titian.* London: Methuen, [1910]. (Classics of Art Series.)
Robinson, Lennox. *Ireland's Abbey Theatre: A History, 1899-1951.* London: Sidgwick & Jackson, 1951.
————. "Irish Dramatic Costume," in *Robes of Thespis,* ed. Rupert Mason, George Sheringham and R. Boyd Morrison. London: Ernest Benn, 1923, pp. 35-39.
Rollins, Cyril and R. John Wits, eds. *The D'Oyle Carte Opera Company in Gilbert and Sullivan Operas: A Record of Productions, 1875-1961.* London: Michael Joseph, 1962.
Rosenfeld, Sybil. *A Short History of Scene Design in Great Britain.* Oxford: Basil Blackwell, 1973.
————. "Charles Ricketts' designs for the Theatre." *Theatre Notebook* 35, no. 1 (1981), 12-17.
Ross, Robert. *Friend of Friends.* Edited by Margery Ross. London: Jonathon Cape, 1952.
Rothenstein, William. *Men and Memories: Recollections.* 3 vols. London: Faber & Faber, 1931-39. (Volume 3 issued under separate title, *Since Fifty.*)
Rowell, George. *The Victorian Theatre: A Survey.* Oxford: Clarendon Press, 1967.
Ruskin, John. *Selections and Essays.* Edited by Frederick William Roe. New York: Scribner, 1918.

Rutherston, Albert Daniel. *Sixteen Designs for the Theatre*. London: Oxford University Press, 1928.

Saddlemyer, Ann. "The Heroic Discipline of the Looking-Glass: W.B. Yeats' Search for Dramatic Design," in *The World of W.B. Yeats: Essays in Perspective*, rev. ed. Edited by Robin Skelton and Ann Saddlemyer. Seattle: University of Washington Press, 1967.

_____. *J.M. Synge and Modern Comedy*. Dublin: Dolmen Press, 1968.

_____. *Theatre Business: The Correspondence of the First Abbey Theatre Directors: William Butler Yeats, Lady Gregory and J.M. Synge*. Gerrard's Cross, Buckinghamshire: Colin Smythe, 1982.

Scarisbrick, Diana. "Charles Ricketts and his Designs for Jewellery." *Apollo* 116 (Sept. 1982), 163-69.

Shattuck, Roger. *The Banquet Years: The Origin of the Avant-Garde in France: 1885 to World War I*. London: Faber & Faber, 1959.

Shaw, George Bernard. *Collected Letters, 1874-1910*. Edited by Dan H. Laurence. 2 vols. London: Max Reinhardt, the Bodley Head, 1965-72.

_____. *Collected Plays with their Prefaces*, general ed. Dan H. Laurence. London: Max Reinhardt, the Bodley Head, 1970.

_____. *Florence Farr, Bernard Shaw, W.B. Yeats; Letters*. Edited by Clifford Box. New York: Dodd, Mead & Co., 1942.

_____. *Our Theatre in the Nineties*. 3 vols. London: Constable, 1932.

_____. *Shaw: An Autobiography*. Edited by Stanley Weintraub. 2 vols. London: Max Reinhardt, the Bodley Head, 1970.

_____. *Shaw: The Critical Heritage*. Edited by T.F. Evans. London: Routledge & Kegan Paul, 1976.

_____. *Shaw on Theatre*. Edited by E.J. West. New York: Hill & Wang, 1958.

Sheringham, George and James Laver. *Design in the Theatre*. With literary contributions by E. Gordon Craig, Charles B. Cochrane and Nigel Playfair. London: The Studio Limited, 1927.

Short, Ernest. *Theatrical Cavalcade*. London: Eyre & Spottiswoode, 1942.

_____. *Sixty Years of Theatre*. London: Eyre & Spottiswoode, 1951.

Skelton, Robin and Ann Saddlemyer. *The World of W.B. Yeats: Essays in Perspective,* revised ed. Seattle: University of Washington Press, 1967.

Skene, Reg. *The Cuchulain Plays of W.B. Yeats*. London: Macmillan, 1974.

Southern, Richard. *Changeable Scenery*. London: Faber & Faber, 1951.

Spencer, Charles. *Léon Bakst*. New York: St. Martin's Press, 1973.

Sprigge, Elizabeth. *Sybil Thorndike Casson*. London: Gollantz, 1971.

Stephenson, Anthony. "The Impossibilists: Alternatives to the Commercial Theatre in London: 1890-1914." Ph.D. diss., University of Toronto, 1975.

Stokes, John. *Resistible Theatres*. London: Elek, 1972.

Sturgeon, Mary. *Michael Field*. London: Harrap, 1922.

Sutton, Denys. "A Neglected Virtuoso—Charles Ricketts." *Apollo* 83 (Feb. 1966), 138-47.

Symons, Arthur. *Plays, Acting and Music*. London: Duckworth, 1903.

_____. *Studies in Seven Arts*. London: Constable, 1906.

_____. *The Symbolic Movement in Literature*. London: Heinemann, 1899.

Synge, John Millington. *The Collected Letters of John Millington Synge*. Edited by Ann Saddlemyer, vol. I, 1871-1907. Oxford: Oxford University Press, 1983.

_____. *Collected Works: Plays*. 2 vols. Edited by Ann Saddlemyer. London: Oxford University Press, 1968. (Vols. III and IV, general ed. Robin Skelton).

_____. *Letters to Molly*. Edited by Ann Saddlemyer. Cambridge, Mass.: Harvard University Press, 1971.

_____. *Some Letters of J.M. Synge to Lady Gregory and W.B. Yeats*. Edited by Ann Saddlemyer. Dublin: Cuala Press, 1971.

Taylor, John Russell. *The Rise of the Well-Made Play.* London: Methuen, 1967.

Terry, Ellen and Bernard Shaw. *Ellen Terry and Bernard Shaw: A Correspondence.* Edited by Christopher St. John. 2nd ed. London: Reinhardt & Evans, 1949.

Trewin, J.C. *Sybil Thorndike.* London: Rockliff, 1955.

Unterecker, John. *Reader's Guide to William Butler Yeats.* New York: Noonday Press, 1959.

Ure, Peter. *Yeats the Playwright: A Commentary: Character and Design in the Major Plays.* London: Routledge & Kegan Paul, 1963.

Vernon, Frank. *Modern Stage Production.* London: "The Stage," 1923.

_____. *The Twentieth Century Theatre.* London: Harrap, 1924.

Volbach, R. *Adolphe Appia: Prophet of the Modern Theatre.* Middleton, Conn.: Wesleyan University Press, 1968.

Walbrook, H.M. *J.M. Barrie and the Theatre.* London: F.V. White, 1922.

Walkley, A.B. *Drama and Life.* London: Methuen, 1907.

Wall, Vincent. *Bernard Shaw: Pygmalion to Many Players.* Ann Arbor: University of Michigan Press, 1973.

Watson, Ernest Bradlee. *Sheridan to Robertson: A Study of the Nineteenth Century London Stage.* Cambridge, Mass.: Harvard University Press, 1926.

Weintraub, Stanley. *Beardsley.* London: W.H. Allen, 1967.

_____. *Journey to Heartbreak: The Crucible Years of Bernard Shaw.* New York: Weybright & Talley, 1971.

White, Colin. *Edmund Dulac.* London: Studio Vista, 1976.

Wilde, Oscar. *Complete Works.* Edited by Vyvyan Holland. 2nd rev. ed. London: Collins, 1966.

_____. *Letters.* Edited by Rupert Hart-Davis. New York: Harcourt, Brace & World, 1962.

Williams, Raymond. *Drama from Ibsen to Brecht.* London: Chatto & Windus, 1968.

Wilson, A.E. *The Edwardian Theatre.* London: Barker, 1951.

Wilson, Edmund. *Axël Castle.* New York: Scribner, 1943.

Yeats, W.B. *Autobiographies.* London: Macmillan, 1955.

_____. *Essays and Introductions.* New York: Macmillan, 1961.

_____. *Ideas of Good and Evil.* London: A.H. Bullen, 1907.

_____. *Collected Poems.* London: Macmillan, 1950.

_____. *The King's Threshold and On Baile's Strand.* London: A.H. Bullen, 1904.

_____. *The Letters of W.B. Yeats.* Edited by Allan Wade. New York: Macmillan, 1955.

_____. "The Play, the Player and the Scene," *Samhain,* Dec. 1904.

_____. *Plays for an Irish Theatre.* With designs by Gordon Craig. London: A.H. Bullen, 1911.

_____. *Uncollected Prose.* 2 vols. Edited by John P. Frayne and Colton Johnson. London: Macmillan, 1975.

_____. *The Variorum Edition of the Plays of W.B. Yeats.* Edited by Russell K. Alspach. and Catherine C. Alspach. New York: Macmillan, 1966.

_____. *The Variorum Edition of the Poems of W.B. Yeats.* Edited by Peter Allt and Russell K. Alspach. New York: Macmillan, 1957.

_____. *W.B. Yeats and T. Sturge Moore: Their Correspondence, 1901-1937.* Edited by Ursula Bridge. London: Routledge & Kegan Paul, 1953.

Index